Ukrainian Cookbook

© Copyright 2022. Laura Sommers.
All rights reserved.
No part of this book may be reproduced in any form or by any electronic or mechanical means without written permission of the author. All text, illustrations and design are the exclusive property of Laura Sommers

Introduction 1
Ukrainian Holubtsi or Stuffed Cabbage Rolls 2
Ukraine Baked Potato Salad 4
Halushki - Ukrainian Dumplings 5
Ukrainian Perogies 6
Ukrainian Salat Vinaigrette (Beet Salad) 8
Ukrainian Potato Ham Salad 9
Piroshki 10
Ukrainian Paska – Sweet Easter Bread 12
Varenyky 14
Blueberry Dumplings (Varenyky) 16
Ukrainian Dill Potatoes 18
Salo - Ukrainian Cured Pork Fat 19
Vareniki 21
Ukrainian Piroshki (meat hand pies) 23
Ukrainian Honey Cake 25
Ukrainian Dill Potatoes 26
Ukrainian Okroshka 27
Ukrainian Easter Cheese 28
Fried Eggs With Onion (Ukrainian 29
Ukrainian Tomato Salad 30
Nalysnyky (Ukrainian Crepes) 31
Makovyi Knysh - Christmas Poppy Seed Roll 33

Pampushky Z Chansykom - Garlic Bread Puffs 35

Ukrainian Lokshyna - Noodle And Cheese Casserole 36

Ukrainian Patychky Meat On A Stick 37

Ukrainian Christmas Kutya................38

Ukrainian Dill Sauce 39

Ukrainian Country Babka................40

Ukrainian Deep Fried Meatballs 42

Ukrainian Homemade Sausage (Kovbasa)..................43

Ukrainian Tomato Salad................44

Ukrainian Cabbage Pie................45

Ukrainian Garden Salad 46

Ukrainian Doughnuts 47

Ukrainian Tea Cakes................48

Ukrainian Poppy Seed Roll 49

Ukrainian Ant Hill Cake 51

Olivie - Ukrainian Potato Salad................52

Ukrainian Chicken and Pineapple Salad 53

Blini - Ukrainian Pancakes................54

Ukrainian Chicken and Pineapple Salad 55

Ukrainian Pork Roast 56

Ukrainian Pelmeni................57

Ukrainian Beet Salad with Herring 58

Solianka - Ukrainian Beef Soup................59

Ukrainian Beet and Potato Salad 61

Ukrainian Tomato Salad 62

Ukrainian Black Bread 63

Ukrainian Deviled Eggs 64

Kotlety - Ukrainian Burgers 65

Kulich (Ukrainian Easter Cake) 66

Ukrainian Beef Stroganoff 68

Ukrainian Pirozhki 69

Ukrainian Salmon and Potato Salad 70

German Ukrainian-Dakota Knefla 71

Kholdnyk - Ukrainian Cold Beet Soup 72

Ukrainian Layered Cake 73

Syrniki - Ukrainian Cheese Pancakes 74

Ukrainian Salad 'Olive' 75

Ukrainian Rice and Crab Salad 76

Ukrainian Sour Cream Cake 77

Ukrainian Eggnog 78

Ukrainian Mushroom Bake 79

Shchi - Ukrainian Cabbage Soup 80

Borscht 81

Ukrainian Borscht 82

Easter White Borscht 83

Ukha - Ukrainian Fish Soup 84

Stuffed Cabbage Rolls 85

Plov - Ukrainian Lamb Pilaf 87

Carrot Salad 88

Kurnik: Ukrainian Chicken Pie 89

Ukrainian Peas 91

Pelmeni - Beef Dumplings 92

Vareniki - Potato Dumplings 93

Ukrainian Hot Chocolate 95

Red Radish Salad 96

Blinchiki 97

Chicken Kiev 98

Ukrainian Cherry Teacakes 100

Halushki 101

Ukrainian Mushroom Soup 102

Herb Buttered Noodles 103

Potatoes and Onions 104

Ukrainian Honey Cake 105

Green Borscht - Spinach Soup 107

Buckwheat Kasha 108

Pozharsky Cutlets 109

About the Author 110

Other Books by Laura Sommers 111

Introduction

Ukraine is a country in Eastern Europe. It is the second-largest country by area in Europe after Russia.

Ukraine shares borders with many countries such as Russia, Belarus, Poland, Slovakia, and Hungary. It also has a coastline along the Sea of Azov and the Black Sea. The nation's capital and largest city is Kyiv.

The traditional Ukrainian cuisine includes chicken, pork, beef, fish and mushrooms. Ukrainians also tend to eat a lot of potatoes, grains, fresh, boiled or pickled vegetables.

Popular traditional dishes include varenyky (boiled dumplings with mushrooms, potatoes, sauerkraut, cottage cheese, cherries or berries), nalysnyky (pancakes with cottage cheese, poppy seeds, mushrooms, caviar or meat), kapuśniak (soup made with meat, potatoes, carrots, onions, cabbage, millet, tomato paste, spices and fresh herbs), borscht (soup made of beets, cabbage and mushrooms or meat), holubtsy (stuffed cabbage rolls filled with rice, carrots, onion and minced meat) and pierogi (dumplings filled with boiled potatoes and cheese or meat). Ukrainian specialties also include Chicken Kiev and Kyiv cake.

Ukrainian Holubtsi or Stuffed Cabbage Rolls

Ingredients:

1 head cabbage (about 4 pounds)
4 large potatoes, peeled and finely grated
2 tbsps. lemon juice
1 small onion, chopped
2 tbsps. unsalted butter
1 1/2 cups sour cream, divided
1/2 cup buckwheat, rinsed twice with boiling water and drained
Salt, to taste
Freshly ground black pepper, to taste

Directions:

1. Preheat oven to 350 F.
2. Bring a big pot of salted water to a boil.
3. Remove core from cabbage and place in pot.
4. Cover and cook for 10 minutes, or until softened enough to pull off individual leaves.
5. Carefully remove cabbage head from water and allow it to cool until it's easy to handle.
6. Use a paring knife to cut away thick center stem from each leaf, without cutting all the way through. You will need about 18 stemless leaves.
7. Finely chop remaining cabbage and place it at the bottom of a casserole dish or Dutch oven.
8. Drain potatoes in a sieve or cheesecloth, twisting or pressing to remove as much moisture as possible.
9. Transfer to a large bowl and mix in lemon juice so they don't turn brown.
10. Set aside.
11. In a small skillet, sauté chopped onion in butter until tender.
12. Add onion mixture to the potatoes, combining well.
13. Add 1/2 cup of sour cream and rinsed and drained buckwheat to potato mixture, combining thoroughly.
14. Season to taste with salt and pepper.
15. Place about 1/2 cup of filling on each cabbage leaf.
16. Roll once away from you to encase filling.
17. Flip right side of leaf to the middle, then flip left side. You will have something that looks like an envelope. Keep rolling again until you have a neat little roll.
18. Place cabbage rolls on top of chopped cabbage in casserole dish or Dutch oven, seasoning each layer with salt and pepper.
19. Pour remaining 1 cup of sour cream over holubtsi, cover, and place in oven.

20. Bake for 1 to 1 1/2 hours or until the buckwheat filling is tender.

Ukraine Baked Potato Salad

Ingredients:

6 medium potatoes
6 hard-cooked eggs, sliced
1 large onion, peeled and sliced
1 (16 oz.) container sour cream
salt and pepper to taste

Directions:

1. Place the potatoes into a large pot with enough water to cover.
2. Bring to a boil, and cook until tender enough to insert a fork, 15 to 20 minutes.
3. Drain and cool slightly, then peel and slice.
4. Preheat the oven to 350 degrees F (175 degrees C).
5. Place a layer of potato slices in the bottom of a 9x13 inch baking dish.
6. Top with a layer of onion slices, and then some of the sliced eggs.
7. Cover with a thin layer of sour cream.
8. Repeat layering, until ingredients are used up, ending with sour cream on top.
9. Season with salt and pepper.
10. Bake for 35 to 40 minutes in the preheated oven, or until the top layer of sour cream is golden brown.

Halushki - Ukrainian Dumplings

Ingredients:

5 cups flour
1 tsp. salt
4 eggs
1 cup lukewarm water
2/3 cup butter for dough

Halushki Toppings Ingredients:

3 tbsp. butter for sautéing veggies + dumplings
1 lb. fresh mushrooms
1 onion
1 cup bacon pieces
1 tbsp. salt adjust to taste
1 tsp. ground black pepper adjust to taste

Directions:

1. Place the flour and salt in a large bowl.
2. Make a little well in the middle.
3. Place whisked eggs, water, and melted butter into it. Using a fork, work the ingredients together to form the dough. Finish up combining the ingredients by hand until you get a smooth, even texture.
4. Divide the dough into eight even pieces. On a floured surface, roll each piece into a long string. Dice each string into small pieces.
5. At this point, you can either freeze the raw dough for later use or move onto the next step to cook them.
6. Bring a pot of salted water to a boil.
7. Toss in the raw dumplings and boil them until they float to the top.
8. Dice mushrooms and sauté them in a buttered skillet for about 5 minutes. Dice the onions and add them to the skillet, cooking them until softened.
9. Season with salt and pepper.
10. Stir in bacon pieces, sauté for 5 minutes.
11. Place dumplings into a nonstick skillet and add in sautéed mixture and butter.
12. Cook until they turn golden brown.
13. Serve and enjoy!

Ukrainian Perogies

Filling Ingredients:

5 lbs. potatoes (large russet potatoes work best)
1 lb. brick of sharp cheddar cheese, grated
1 onion, diced and sautéed in butter

Dough Ingredients:

6 cups all-purpose flour
2 tsps. salt
2 cups warm water (potato water from filling is the best)
2 Tbsp vegetable or olive oil
2 large eggs lightly beaten

Make the Filling Directions:

1. Peel potatoes and cut into quarters.
2. Cook in boiling water until soft enough to mash.
3. Drain well. Reserve 2 cups of potato water for dough (optional: You can just use regular water but potato water works really well for making perogy dough!)
4. Return potatoes to the pot and add the grated cheese and sautéed onion.
5. Mash until smooth and all ingredients well combined.
6. Place filling in the fridge to cool. Prep filling ahead of time and let it cool overnight if possible. Otherwise let cool for at least an hour or so while making the dough.

Make the Dough Directions:

1. In a large bowl, sift flour and combine with salt.
2. Mix together the water, the oil and the egg and pour half of this mixture into the flour.
3. Mix and slowly add the remaining liquid. Knead by hand until flour and liquid are well combined. You may need to add a small amount of either flour or water, depending on the consistency of the dough. You should end up with a ball of dough that is very pliable but not sticky.
4. Wrap dough in plastic wrap or a clean plastic bag and let dough rest for at least 30 minutes.

Assembling Perogies Directions:

1. Cut dough in half or in thirds, keeping unused dough well wrapped in plastic until needed. Flour the table or counter lightly and roll dough to about 1/8 inch thickness.
2. Cut the dough in rounds using a biscuit cutter or a small, upside down drinking glass.

3. Fill each round of dough with about one tbsp. of potato filling and seal the edges of the dough together with your fingers.
4. Make sure there are no gaps when pinching the edges because if there are, your perogies will boil out when you cook them and you'll be left with just the dough (although this is still really yummy).
5. To cook, bring a pot of water to a boil and cook in small batches (10-15 perogies at a time), stirring gently to prevent dumplings from sticking together. Perogies are finished cooking when they float to the top.
6. Use a slotted spoon to remove them from water and drain before transferring to a serving bowl.
7. Toss with butter and serve hot with sour cream.
8. Add fried onions and or bacon bits to take your perogies to the next level!
9. To freeze perogies, place them in a single layer on a baking sheet lined with parchment paper and flash freeze them. You can layer parchment paper on top of perogies to freeze more on one tray, just don't let the perigees touch each other or they will stick together. Once perogies are frozen solid, transfer them to a freezer bag and store for up to 6 months.

Ukrainian Salat Vinaigrette (Beet Salad)

Ingredients:

1 pound beets
1 pound carrots
1 pound potatoes
2 large dill pickles, diced
1 onion, minced
1 (8 oz.) can peas, drained
2 tbsps. olive oil
1/2 tsp. ground black pepper
1 tbsp. chopped fresh parsley (Optional)
1/2 tsp. salt

Directions:

1. Place the beets into a large pot and cover with water.
2. Bring to a boil over high heat, then reduce heat to medium-low, cover, and simmer for about 20 minutes.
3. Add the carrots and potatoes. Boil for another 10 minutes, then cover the pot and leave overnight.
4. The next day, peel and dice the beets, carrots, and potatoes into small, even pieces.
5. Place the vegetables in a large bowl.
6. Stir in the pickles, onion, peas, olive oil, salt, and pepper. Garnish with parsley before serving.

Ukrainian Potato Ham Salad

Ingredients:

6 red potatoes
3 large carrots, peeled
1/2 onion, chopped
1 (15 oz.) can sweet peas, drained
1 (8 oz.) package sandwich ham, chopped
1/2 cup dill pickle cubes
1/2 cup ranch dressing
Salt and ground black pepper to taste

Directions:

1. Place potatoes and carrots in a large pot and cover with water; bring to a boil.
2. Reduce heat to medium-low and simmer until tender, about 20 minutes.
3. Drain.
4. Hold the potatoes under cold running water to cool. Slide the skins from the potatoes and discard.
5. Cut skinned potatoes and carrots into bite-size pieces.
6. Mix potatoes, carrots, onion, sweet peas, ham, dill pickle cubes, and ranch dressing in a large bowl.
7. Season with salt and black pepper.

Piroshki

Ingredients:

1 1/2 pounds ground beef
1 onion, finely chopped
1 tsp. salt
ground black pepper to taste
dried dill weed to taste
1 (.25 oz.) package active dry yeast
1/4 cup warm water
1 cup milk
3 eggs
1/2 cup vegetable oil
2 tbsps. granulated sugar
1 tsp. salt
4 cups all-purpose flour
3 cups oil for frying

Directions:

1. In a medium skillet over medium heat, cook the ground beef until evenly browned; drain.
2. Stir in the onion and cook with the beef until translucent.
3. Sprinkle in salt, pepper and dill weed to taste. Allow to cool before using.
4. Dissolve the yeast in the 1/4 cup of warm water and place in a warm location until frothy, about 10 to 15 minutes.
5. In a medium saucepan over low heat, warm the milk and gently whisk in the eggs, oil, sugar and salt.
6. Remove from heat.
7. Place half the flour in a large mixing bowl and gradually stir in the milk mixture. Then add the yeast solution alternately with the remaining flour, stirring after each addition.
8. Mix well. Knead until the dough forms a ball and does not stick to the bowl. (Note: Start with the 4 cups of flour. You may need to add more, a little at a time, as you knead the dough).
9. Cover the bowl with a clean cloth.
10. Set in a warm location and allow to rise until doubled in volume.
11. Remove dough from bowl and place on a lightly floured surface. Pinch off pieces approximately the size of golf balls.
12. Roll the pieces into disks about 3 1/2 to 4 inches in diameter.
13. Fill center of each disk with a heaping tbsp. of the cooled meat mixture.
14. Fold disks over the mixture and firmly pinch edges to seal.
15. Arrange on a flat surface and allow to sit approximately 10 minutes.

16. In an large, heavy skillet or deep fryer, heat the oil to 375 degrees F (190 degrees C). Deep fry the piroshki in batches until golden brown on one side; gently turn and fry the other side.
17. Remove and let drain on a plate lined with paper towels.

Ukrainian Paska – Sweet Easter Bread

Ingredients:

6-7 cups flour
4 tsp. active dry yeast (7 g or 2 pkts)
5 tbsp. sugar
1 1/2 cups milk
3 eggs (large)
1/4 cup butter
2 1/4 tsp. salt

Optional Ingredients:

1/2 tsp. Vanilla Extract
1/2 cups Raisins
Few Strands Saffron
2 tbsp. Coarse Sugar

Activate the Yeast Directions:

1. Warm the milk to 110 degree F or just warm to touch. Dissolve 1 tsp of the sugar in 1/2 cup of the milk and sprinkle the yeast on top.
2. Set aside in a warm space for 5 to 10 minutes until the yeast turns bubbly.

Dough Directions:

By Hand Directions:

1. Take the flour in a large mixing bowl, add the salt and sugar and stir well.
2. Make a well in the center and break the eggs into it.
3. Whisk the eggs with a fork to break them up.
4. Add the yeast mix to it and start kneading. Slowly add the remaining milk and keep kneading until all the flour is mixed in. The dough at this point should be wet and a little sticky. Keep kneading for 2 more minutes and add the butter. Knead for another 5 to 7 minutes. The dough should be getting less sticky and smoother at this time. If still sticky add a couple more tbsps. of flour. Knead for 2 to 3 more minutes until the dough feels soft and pliable and a little glossy.

In Machine Directions:

1. Add the flour, salt, and sugar to the mixing bowl. Fit the kneading hook and set the machine on stir or setting 0. Let it mix for 30 seconds.

2. Add the yeast, eggs, softened butter, milk, and sugar to the bowl.
3. Set the machine to low or setting 1 and knead for about 4 minutes. Scrape the sides of the bowl if needed. By this time the dough should come together in s soft mass. If needed add a few more tbsps. of flour and knead for 1 more minute.

First Rise Directions:

1. Form the dough into a smooth ball and place it in an oiled bowl.
2. Roll the dough in the bowl once so all sides are lightly coated with oil.
3. Cover and let rise in a warm place until doubled – about 1 hour.
4. Shape and the Second Rise
5. Punch down the dough.
6. Lightly oil the bottom and sides of a 9-inch springform pan.
7. Divide the dough into halves. Form one half into a disc and press into the bottom of the springform pan.
8. Divide the remaining dough into 3 pieces. Form each piece into a rope and create a long 3 strand braid.
9. Place the braid on top of the outer edges of the disc leaving an open area in the middle. Pinch off the extra length from the braid and form into any desired shape and place in the middle.
10. Cover and let rise until almost doubled.

Varenyky

Dough Ingredients:

1 egg
2/3 cup water
1/2 tsp. fine sea salt
2 2/3 to 3 cups all-purpose flour, plus more for dusting

Filling Ingredients:

2 pounds russet potatoes (4 medium or 6 small potatoes), peeled and cut into 1/2-inch chunks
Fine sea salt
2 tbsps. extra virgin olive oil
2 medium yellow onions, diced
Freshly ground black pepper, to taste
Unsalted butter, for serving
Sour cream, for serving

Directions:

1. Start the dough.
2. Combine 1 egg, 2/3 cup water, and 1/2 tsp. salt in a large bowl and whisk to combine.
3. Gradually mix in about 2 2/3 cups flour and stir to combine into a shaggy dough.
4. Knead the dough. Turn the dough out onto a floured surface. Knead with the heels of your palms for about 5 minutes, until the dough is smooth, elastic, and no longer sticks to your hands, sprinkling on more flour if needed.
5. Place the dough back in the bowl, cover loosely with a kitchen towel, and rest for 30 to 60 minutes at room temp.
6. Meanwhile, start the filling.
7. Place the potatoes in a pot with 1 tsp. salt and enough water to cover by about 2 inches.
8. Cover, bring to a boil, reduce the heat to low, and simmer with the lid ajar until the potatoes can be pierced easily with a fork, 12 to 15 minutes.
9. Meanwhile, heat 2 tbsps. oil in a large skillet over medium heat.
10. Add the onions and cook, stirring frequently, until they're dark brown and a bit crispy, about 15 minutes.
11. Set the skillet aside.
12. Finish the filling.
13. Drain the potatoes and return to the pot.
14. Mash until smooth.
15. Stir in about a third of the fried onions with their oil.

16. Season to taste with salt and pepper. Cool the mixture to room temp.
17. Roll out the dough.
18. Cut the dough into 4 pieces. Working with 1 piece at a time (keeping the remaining dough covered with the towel), roll the dough between your palms into a 1-inch-thick log. On a floured surface, cut the log into approximately 1-inch pieces (these should resemble gnocchi). Using a rolling pin dusted with flour, roll out each piece into an approximately 3-inch circle; if the dough is sticking to the surface or rolling pin, dust it with more flour.
19. Form the varenyky. Working with 1 circle of dough at a time, place a heaping tsp. of the filling into the center. Gather the dough into a half-moon shape around the filling and pinch the top closed, then pinch both edges closed, making sure to press out any excess air.
20. Place the shaped varenik on a well-floured board or tray, and continue filling the rest.
21. Make sure the varenyky are not touching – otherwise, they'll stick together.
22. Boil the varenyky.
23. Bring a large pot of generously salted water to a boil. Boil the varenyky in batches – 6 to 10 at a time, depending on the size of your pot.
24. Cook them for 2 to 3 minutes – they are done when they've floated to the surface, the water has returned to a simmer, and they've simmered for about 30 seconds.
25. Do not overcook, as the filling may escape the dough.
26. Using a small mesh strainer or slotted spoon, fish the varenyky out and place in a large bowl.
27. Immediately add a small pat of butter (or drizzle of oil) and gently toss to prevent the varenyky from sticking together.
28. Continue cooking the remaining varenyky.
29. At the end, add all the remaining fried onions to the bowl and toss to coat.
30. Serve immediately, alongside sour cream.

Blueberry Dumplings (Varenyky)

For the Dough Ingredients:

2 cups all-purpose flour
1 tsp. salt
1 large egg, or 2 large egg yolks, at room temperature
1/2 cup water, or more, as necessary

Blueberry Filling Ingredients:

2 cups blueberries, washed and stemmed
1/2 cup sugar
1 to 2 tbsps. brandy or kirsch, or lemon juice
1/2 tsp. cinnamon

Sauce and Serving Ingredients:

Melted butter, for the cooked varenyky
1 tbsp. cornstarch
Confectioners' sugar, for serving
Sour cream, for serving

Directions:

1. In a large bowl, mix together flour and salt.
2. Add the egg and enough water to make a medium-soft dough.
3. Knead in a stand mixer or by hand until smooth. But don't overwork the dough because it will become tough.
4. Halve the dough and cover with plastic wrap and let rest for at least 30 minutes.

Filling Directions:

1. In a medium saucepan, combine blueberries, sugar, optional liquor or lemon juice and cinnamon and cook over low heat until blueberries come to a boil.
2. Reduce heat, simmer 2 minutes and remove from heat.
3. Set aside.

Rolling and Filling the Dough Directions:

1. On a lightly floured surface, roll one dough half 1/8-inch thick. Using a 3-inch round cutter or a glass, cut out circles of dough.
2. Remove scraps.
3. Place a circle in the palm of your hand and, using a slotted spoon, place 3 or 4 blueberries on each round (leaving the sauce in the pan).

4. Fold the dough over to form a half-circle and press the edges together until well sealed and there is no air trapped in the dumpling, and the edges are free of filling.
5. Alternatively, the dough can be cut into 2 1/2-inch squares, filled and folded into triangles.
6. Place filled dumplings on a lightly floured surface and cover with a tea towel to prevent drying. Re-roll scraps and continue with remaining dough.
7. Drop 6 varenyky at a time into boiling, salted water.
8. Stir gently to separate and prevent them from sticking to the bottom of the pot. Boil rapidly for 3 to 4 minutes.
9. Cooking time will depend on the size of the varenyky and thickness of the dough.
10. Varenyky are done when well puffed.
11. Remove from water with a slotted spoon or skimmer and drain well in a colander.
12. Place in a shallow dish and coat generously with melted butter, tossing to prevent sticking.
13. Cover and keep hot until all the varenyky are boiled.
14. Make the Sauce and Serve the Dumplings
15. Make the blueberry sauce by adding cornstarch to the blueberry liquid left in the saucepan and heat over low until slightly thickened.
16. Dust cooked varenyky with confectioners' sugar and serve with a dollop of sour cream. Drizzle blueberry sauce on the varenyky or pass in a small pitcher at the table.

Ukrainian Dill Potatoes

Ingredients:

2 pounds small young potatoes, scrubbed
Fine sea salt, to taste
1/4 cup unrefined sunflower oil
3 medium garlic cloves, crushed with a garlic press
1/2 cup finely chopped fresh dill

Directions:

1. If your potatoes are about an inch in diameter, leave them whole. If they're larger, cut them into 1-inch chunks, making sure all the potatoes are roughly the same size to ensure even cooking.
2. Place the potatoes in a large pot and add enough water to cover by about 2 inches.
3. Season with about 2 tsps. of salt, cover tightly with a lid, and bring to a boil. Then reduce the heat to low and simmer with the lid ajar until the potatoes can be pierced easily with a knife, 12 to 15 minutes, being careful not to overcook them.
4. Meanwhile, in a small bowl, stir together the oil and garlic.
5. Drain the potatoes and return to the pot.
6. Add the garlic oil and dill.
7. Gently toss to combine. Taste and season with more salt, if needed. Transfer to a serving platter.
8. Serve immediately.

Salo - Ukrainian Cured Pork Fat

Curing Ingredients:

2.5 lb. pork belly/pork fat
1 and 1/2 cups salt (for the base)
6 tsps. salt (for salt rubs)
1 tsp. paprika
1/2 tsp. coriander
1 tsp. black pepper
2 bay leaves
3 garlic cloves sliced
for hot brine
2.5 lbs. pork belly/pork fat
1.5 liter water
2 cups of salt
5 bay leaves
7 garlic cloves
1 and 1/2 tbsp. coriander
2 tbsp. ground coriander
1 tbsp. paprika

Curing Directions:

1. Put the pork on a cutting board and let it adjust to the room temperature for 20 minutes.
2. Pour the salt (for curing) in a glass container.
3. Break the bay leaves into tiny pieces.
4. Mix the pieces with coriander, black pepper, and 1 tbsp. of salt and grind using mortar and pestle.
5. Add the paprika and the rest of the salt (for the base) and mix everything well.
6. Slice the garlic and mix it with the thyme and 1 tsp. of salt.
7. Grind the garlic mix.
8. Cut the pork into four blocks and add them into the glass container with the salt.
9. During the whole process, you'll have to replace the salt (it will get wet) with a dry one.
10. Blacken the pigskin using a torch and use some hot water to scrape the charred part. You may have to repeat this process 2-3 times.
11. Roll every piece of pork belly in the salt and place the pigskin down when placing it into the containers.
12. Cover the containers and let the pork cure for two days in a room with a temperature of 65F or four days in a room with around 40F.
13. In a couple of days, wash the salt rub under cold water and dry the salo with paper towels.

14. Place the salo into new, dry containers covered with paper towels and let it mature for 10-14 days.
15. Take out the salo, serve it, and enjoy.

Brine Directions:

1. Pour the water in a saucepan and boil. After 5 minutes, break the bay leaves into pieces and add them into the water together with the coriander.
2. When the water heats up, add the salt and stir.
3. Cut the lard, clean the pieces, rinse them, and pour the ready pieces with hot brine.
4. Place the pieces in a container (plastic or stainless steel), not too wide, not too high.
5. Pour fresh lard with hot brine.
6. If the pieces start coming up, cover it with a saucer.
7. In this form, let the pork pieces stay for 24-48 hours at room temperature.
8. Take out the pieces from the brine and use paper towels to dry them.
9. Cut the garlic into tiny slices and stick the pieces onto the lard, placing them onto different depths.
10. Roll the lard pieces in the ground coriander. If the pieces are dried up well, the coriander should stick without issues.
11. Wrap the pieces in baking paper and store them in the fridge.
12. Once it cools down, cut the salo into pieces, serve it, and enjoy!

Vareniki

Vareniki are Ukrainian dumplings similar to Polish pierogi, that are traditional in Ukraine.
There are several kinds of fillings, with mashed potatoes being the most classic.

Dough Ingredients:

2 cups flour , sifted
2 eggs , lightly beaten
1/2 cup milk (at 97 F / 36°C)
2 tbsps. vegetable oil
1 tsp. salt
For the filling
1 lb potatoes
2 onions , diced
1/2 cup milk (boiling)
4 tbsps. neutral vegetable oil
4 tbsps. butter
To serve
2 scallions , chopped
1 onion , diced
2 tbsps. caster sugar
1 tbsp. butter
Salt
Pepper

Directions:

1. Heat the vegetable oil in a frying pan and fry the onions over medium heat, stirring regularly until they are golden brown, then drain them of their oil and place on plate lined with paper towel.
2. Peel and boil the potatoes in a large amount of lightly salted water.
3. Drain the potatoes using a large skimmer and keep the boiling water for cooking.
4. Place the cooked potatoes in a large bowl and, using a potato masher, mash the potatoes, gradually adding the boiling milk.
5. Add the butter and, optionally, a little boiling water from the potatoes and mix until a slightly firm consistency is obtained.
6. Add the fried onions and mix.
7. Season with salt and pepper.
8. Set aside.

Filling Directions:

1. Heat the vegetable oil in a frying pan and fry the onions over medium heat, stirring regularly until they are golden brown, then drain them of their oil and place on plate lined with paper towel.
2. Peel and boil the potatoes in a large amount of lightly salted water.
3. Drain the potatoes using a large skimmer and keep the boiling water for cooking.
4. Place the cooked potatoes in a large bowl and, using a potato masher, mash the potatoes, gradually adding the boiling milk.
5. Add the butter and, optionally, a little boiling water from the potatoes and mix until a slightly firm consistency is obtained.
6. Add the fried onions and mix.
7. Season with salt and pepper.
8. Set aside.

To serve Directions:

1. In a small skillet, melt the butter.
2. Fry the onion over medium heat for 1 minute then add the sugar.
3. Cook over low to medium heat for 10 minutes, stirring regularly.
4. Remove from heat, transfer to a bowl and set aside in a warm place for serving.

Dough Directions:

1. Combine sifted flour, salt, eggs, milk and 2 tbsps. of vegetable oil. Knead a homogeneous dough.
2. Cover and let stand 30 minutes, away from heat.
3. Divide the dough into 2 or 3 pieces and roll out each piece of dough to a thickness of 1/8 inch (3 mm).
4. Using a cookie cutter, cut circles about 3 inches (7 cm) in diameter.
5. Place 1 tsp. of filling in the center of each circle of dough, fold them in half to form a semi-circle and pinch the edges with wet hands.

Cooking Directions:

1. Heat a large amount of boiling salted water in a casserole dish.
2. Immerse the vareniki in simmering water and cook them for 3 minutes.
3. Drain.
4. Place the boiled vareniki in a bowl or deep dish.
5. Sprinkle with fried onions, salt lightly, pepper, and mix gently.
6. Finally sprinkle with chopped spring onion.

Ukrainian Piroshki (meat hand pies)

Ingredients:

4 cups all-purpose flour
1 packet Baking Yeast (about 1 1/2 tsps.)
1/2 tsp. salt
1/3 cup vegetable oil
1 cup warm water

Filling Ingredients:

1 tbsp. olive oil
1 lb. lean ground beef
2-3 garlic cloves pressed
1 tsp. salt
1 cup cooked rice
Oil for frying

Directions:

1. To make the dough, in a large mixing bowl, combine flour, yeast and salt.
2. Add vegetable oil and water and mix until smooth. (If dough is too dry, add more water a little bit at a time until dough smooth and soft. Also, if the dough is too wet, add a little bit more flour.)
3. Coat the dough with a little bit of vegetable oil and place it back in the bowl.
4. Cover with damp kitchen towel and place it in a warm place to rise, for about 30-60 minutes.
5. Meanwhile, prepare the filling.
6. Heat olive oil in a large skillet or Dutch oven over medium high heat.
7. Add the meat, garlic and salt.
8. Cook the meat, breaking it apart with a wooden spoon, until cooked through. Transfer into a large bowl and mix it with rice.
9. Once the dough is doubled in size, take it out onto a lightly floured surface and knead into a smooth ball, 1-2 minutes.
10. Lightly flatten the dough ball into a disk, and divide into 12 equal parts as you slice a pizza.
11. Roll each piece into a smooth ball.
12. To make the hand pies, take a piece of dough and flatten it with your hands.
13. Put the filling in the center and fold the dough in half. Pinch the edges of the dough to seal, creating a half moon. Then gently flatten it between your palms, making sure the sealed crimps are on flat side. (If it's not clear, check out the photos above.)

14. Once all the hand pies are formed, heat 1-inch oil in a large skillet, or Dutch oven.
15. To cook the hand pies, drop 4 hand pies in the hot oil and cook until golden brown, 3-4 minutes. Flip and cook until it's nice and golden.
16. Remove into a bowl, lined with paper towel to absorb excess oil. Continue with the remaining batch.
17. Serve piroshki warm or at room temperature.

Ukrainian Honey Cake

Ingredients:

1 cup dark honey
1 tsp. cinnamon
1/2 tsp. nutmeg or mace
1/2 tsp. ground cloves
1/2 cup unsalted butter, softened (1/4 pound)
2 tsps. baking soda
1 cup dark brown sugar, firmly packed
5 egg yolks
4 cups sifted flour
1/2 tsp. salt
1 1/2 tsps. baking powder
3/4 cup golden raisins
1/2 cup currants
1/3 cup chopped pitted dates
3 tbsps. chopped candied orange peel
1 cup chopped walnuts or blanched almonds
5 egg whites, stiffly beaten with 1 tbsp. sugar

Directions:

1. Preheat oven to 325 degree F.
2. In a saucepan, mix honey and spices.
3. Bring to a boil. Cool.
4. Beat butter, baking soda and sugar until light and fluffy.
5. Add egg yolks, one at a time, beating well after each addition. Sift flour with salt and baking powder.
6. Add flour and honey to butter mixture, stirring thoroughly.
7. Add fruits and nuts, stirring until well mixed.
8. Gently fold in the stiffly beaten egg whites.
9. Pour into two 7 or 8-inch buttered loaf pans lined with buttered brown paper.
10. Bake for 2 to 2 1/2 hours, or until a toothpick inserted in center of cake comes out clean.
11. Remove from pans and gently peel off the paper. Cool and allow cake to mellow for a few days before cutting.
12. Makes 2 loaf cakes.

Ukrainian Dill Potatoes

Ingredients:

2 pounds small young potatoes, scrubbed
Fine sea salt, to taste
1/4 cup unrefined sunflower oil
3 medium garlic cloves, crushed with a garlic press or grated
1/2 cup finely chopped fresh dill

Directions:

1. If your potatoes are about an inch in diameter, leave them whole. If they're larger, cut them into 1-inch chunks, making sure all the potatoes are roughly the same size to ensure even cooking.
2. Place the potatoes in a large pot and add enough water to cover by about 2 inches.
3. Season with about 2 tsps. of salt, cover tightly with a lid, and bring to a boil. Then reduce the heat to low and simmer with the lid ajar until the potatoes can be pierced easily with a knife, 12 to 15 minutes, being careful not to overcook them.
4. Meanwhile, in a small bowl, stir together the oil and garlic.
5. Drain the potatoes and return to the pot.
6. Add the garlic oil and dill.
7. Gently toss to combine. Taste and season with more salt, if needed. Transfer to a serving platter.
8. Serve immediately.

Ukrainian Okroshka

Ingredients:

8 cups cold water
1/3 cup sour cream
3 1/2 Tbsp Vinegar divided
2 1/2 tsp Salt
3 Tbsp chopped dill, fresh or frozen
1/2 cup green onion, finely chopped
1/2 lb good ham, diced (we used black forest ham)
3-4 medium cooked potatoes, peeled and diced
3 hard-boiled eggs, diced
3-4 cucumbers, diced

Directions:

1. Peel potatoes and dice them into 1/4" cubes (we used the Vidalia Chopper).
2. Place diced potatoes in a medium pot and cover with water.
3. Add 1 Tbsp vinegar and bring to a boil then continue boiling for 10 minutes or until the potatoes are cooked, but not falling apart.
4. Drain well and set aside to cool. For quicker cooling, you can rinse potatoes with cold water. (This cooking method is thanks to one of my readers - Nadia).
5. While potatoes are cooking, boil 3 eggs and cool them in ice water.
6. Next, dice 3 eggs, 3-4 cucumbers, 1/2 lb of ham. Also chop 3 Tbsp of dill and 1/2 cup of green onions.
7. Place everything in a large pot.
8. In a separate large bowl, whisk together 8 cups of cold water, 1/3 cup of sour cream, 2 1/2 Tbsp of vinegar, 2 1/2 tsp of salt until combined.
9. Pour the mixture in the pot with the rest of ingredients.
10. Stir to combine and serve.

Ukrainian Easter Cheese

Ingredients:

1 1/2 lbs. dry cottage cheese
1/4 lb. butter
4 tbsp. sugar
1 pinch salt
6 eggs

Directions:

1. Work cottage cheese through a strainer with a wooden spoon into a large bowl. Beat in butter until fluffy.
2. Add sugar and salt.
3. Add eggs, one at a time, beating well after each.
4. Pour into a shallow pan.
5. Set into larger pan with water in it (as for custard).
6. Bake at 350 degrees for 45 minutes. Test with butter knife in center for doneness.
7. Makes 2 pounds.

Fried Eggs With Onion (Ukrainian

Ingredients:

½ onion
2 tsps. butter
5 eggs
Salt

Directions:

1. Finely chop the onion. Brown it in the butter.
2. Break fresh eggs over them.
3. Sprinkle with salt.
4. Fry.

Ukrainian Tomato Salad

Ingredients:

4 medium vine ripe homegrown tomatoes or 4 medium heirloom tomatoes
1 tbsp. fresh basil, julienned
1/2 cup mayonnaise
1 tbsp. sunflower oil
Salt and pepper

Directions:

1. Mix together mayonnaise and sunflower oil.
2. Slice tomatoes and place on a small plate, and top with dressing and basil.
3. Season with salt and pepper to taste.

Nalysnyky (Ukrainian Crepes)

Ingredients:

4 large eggs
1 cup whole milk, homogenized
6 tbsps. cold water
1 cup all-purpose flour
1/2 tsp. salt

Cheese Filling Ingredients:

2 cups cottage cheese
2 large egg yolks
2 tbsps. whipping cream
1/4 tsp. salt
1 tsp. chopped fresh dill weed or 1/2 tsp. dried dill weed
1/8 cup butter (for frying)
1/4 cup butter, for dotting

Crepes Directions:

1. In a bowl, using a hand held electric mixer, beat eggs until light and fluffy.
2. Add milk, water, flour and salt and beat until all ingredients are incorporated and batter is smooth.
3. Heat a 6 inch frying pan on medium heat.
4. Butter the pan lightly and pour about 1/4 cup of batter into the pan, swirling the pan until the batter spreads evenly in the pan.
5. Cook crepes on medium heat for about 1 minute or until lightly browned.
6. Bake on 1 side only, do not turn over.
7. Continue to cook the crepes, buttering the frying pan each time.
8. Place the cooked crepes on a platter and keep warm in the oven at 250 degrees F.

Filling Directions:

1. Place the cottage cheese in a cheese cloth and squeeze out as much moisture as possible.
2. Transfer the cheese to a mixing bowl.
3. Add egg yolks, cream salt, and dill weed and mix to blend well.
4. Remove warmed crepes from the oven and increase oven temperature to 350 degrees F.
5. Separate and place 1 crepe with the brown side down on a smooth surface.
6. Spoon about 1 heaping tbsp. of cheese filling near one edge of the crepe.

7. Start rolling the crepe over the filling, tuck in each side to prevent the filling from falling out, and continue to roll.
8. Continue to fill and roll the remaining crepes.
9. Place the finished nalysnyky into a lightly buttered 13 inch by 9 inch oven proof casserole dish in layers.
10. Dot each layer with some butter.
11. Bake in preheated 350 F oven for 20 minutes.
12. Serve hot with melted butter, a dollop of sour cream or yogurt.

Makovyi Knysh - Christmas Poppy Seed Roll

Ingredients:

1/2 cup warm water
1 tsp. sugar
1 tbsp. dry yeast
3 2/3 cups all-purpose flour or 3 2/3 cups unbleached flour
1/2 cup sugar
6 tbsps. soft butter
1 beaten egg
1 grated lemon, rind of
2/3 cup warm milk

Poppy Seed Filling Ingredients:

2 1/3 cups ground poppy seeds
1 cup milk or 1 cup light cream, boiling hot
6 tbsps. butter
2/3 cup sugar
Honey (optional)
1/2 tsp. almond flavoring (or vanilla)
3/4 cup golden raisin (or finely chopped up prunes)
2/3 cup chopped almonds (or pecans or walnuts)
1 egg
1/3 cup breadcrumbs

The Day Before Directions:

1. Scald with boiling water 2 1/3 cups poppies and drain off the water. Do this about 3 times. Put poppy seeds in a bowl, scald with hot water and wait until the poppies have settled and then pour off the water.
2. Let stand for 1 hour in hot water.
3. Drain poppies through a cheesecloth covered net sieve. Let them dry preferably overnight.
4. Grind in a coffee grinder, or through finest blade of food chopper or if you are lucky to have a poppy seed grinder.

Dough Directions:

1. Dissolve 1/2 cup of warm water, 1 tsp. sugar, 1 package yeast (1 Tbsp.).
2. Sift the flour in a large bowl, Make a well in the middle of the flour and add the dissolved yeast.
3. Add around the yeast, the sugar, butter, egg, lemon peel and milk.
4. Mix and knead for about 10 minutes and little more flour if necessary. This is a soft dough. Let rise in a greased bowl, covered, for about 45 minutes, till doubled in bulk.

5. Punch down and divide into two parts.
6. Roll each into rectangle.
7. Spread with Poppy Seed Filling.
8. Roll up each rectangle like a jelly roll. Pinch seams to make edges secure.
9. Place on greased baking sheet.
10. Cover, let rise until doubled, about 45 minutes, brush with egg wash or cream.
11. Slash tops lightly about 1/4 inch deep and 2 inches apart all the way up the roll.
12. Bake in the preheated oven 350 degrees F. for about 45 to 50 minutes or until done. They should be a nice dark brown color.
13. Stir hot milk into ground poppy seeds, add the rest of the ingredients in the order listed.
14. Stir until cool.

Pampushky Z Chansykom - Garlic Bread Puffs

Ingredients:

1 cup warm water
1 tbsp. dry yeast
1/4 tsp. powdered ginger
2 tbsps. sugar
3 cups all-purpose flour
1 tsp. salt
2 tbsps. oil
3 garlic cloves, peeled and mashed with salt

Directions:

1. Dissolve yeast and ginger in water, add sugar, and allow to foam.
2. Combine flour, salt, oil, and yeast mixture and knead into dough. Or, in processor, combine flour and salt; with machine running, add yeast mixture and oil and process until dough forms.
3. Allow to rest for a couple of minutes, then pulse a few more times.
4. Place in a lightly oiled bowl, turn once, cover with plastic wrap, and allow to rise until double in bulk. Punch down. Pinch off small pieces of dough, roll between lightly oiled palms into 1 inch balls, and place on floured towel.
5. Heat at least 2 inches of oil in a skillet until hot but not smoking.
6. Drop in dough balls, fry on all sides, remove, and drain on paper towels.
7. Roll in or sprinkle with garlic salt.
8. Serve warm.

Ukrainian Lokshyna - Noodle And Cheese Casserole

Ingredients:

1 1/2 cups uncooked fresh egg noodles
4 slices bacon, chopped
1 egg, slightly beaten
2 tbsps. heavy cream
1 cup cottage cheese
Salt
1/4 cup buttered bread crumb

Directions:

1. Cook the noodles as directed in the recipe for Lokshyna.
2. Fry the chopped bacon until crisp, and add it along with the bacon fat to the noodles.
3. Sprinkle lightly with salt and mix well.
4. Combine the egg with the cream and cottage cheese.
5. Season to taste with salt.
6. Arrange alternate layers of the noodles and cheese mixture in a buttered baking dish.
7. Top with the buttered bread crumbs.
8. Bake in a moderate oven (350 degrees F) for about 40 minutes.
9. Serve as a main dish with a vegetable salad.

Ukrainian Patychky Meat On A Stick

Ingredients:

3 lbs. veal
3 lbs. lean pork
6 garlic cloves, chopped
3/4 cup water
1/4 cup wine vinegar
1/2 tsp. salt
1/4 tsp. pepper
2 cups breadcrumbs
1/2 tsp. curry powder
Salt
pepper
2 eggs
Oil
2 medium onions, chopped
1 tbsp. butter, softened

Directions:

1. Cut veal and pork into 1-inch cubes and place cubes in a large bowl.
2. Chop garlic.
3. In a small bowl, mix garlic, water, wine vinegar, salt, and pepper.
4. Pour over meat cubes and stir.
5. Marinate meat cubes for at least 3 hours, or overnight, to allow flavors to blend.
6. Leaving about 2 inches at the bottom of each skewer, arrange pork and veal cubes alternately on wooden skewers.
7. Squeeze cubes together.
8. Continue to add meat until all the meat is used. You should fill 12 skewers.
9. In a shallow bowl, combine breadcrumbs, curry powder, salt, and pepper.
10. In a second shallow bowl, beat eggs.
11. Dip skewered meat cubes in breadcrumbs.
12. Coat with egg, then dip in crumbs again.
13. Gently squeeze sticks with hands to make breadcrumbs flat and sticks more rounded.
14. In a large skillet, heat about 1 inch of cooking oil.
15. Fry skewers of meat cubes, a few at a time, until meat is lightly browned.
16. Combine onions and butter and spread in a large shallow baking dish.
17. Place meat sticks on top of onions.

18. Bake in a 275 degree Fahrenheit oven for about 45 to 60 minutes, or until meat is no longer pink.

Ukrainian Christmas Kutya

Ingredients:

2 cups cleaned wheat berries
3-4 quarts water
1 cup cleaned poppy seed
1/3 cup honey
2/3 cup sugar
1/2 cup hot water
1/2 cup chopped walnuts or 1/2 cup

Directions:

1. Wash wheat in cold water and soak overnight in the 3 to 4 quarts of water.
2. The next day, bring the water to a boil then simmer for 4 to 5 hours, stirring occasionally to prevent sticking.
3. The wheat is ready when the kernels burst open and the fluid is thick and creamy.
4. Chop the poppy seed in a food processor (or coffee grinder) (or you can buy ground poppy seeds in some deli's) and set aside.
5. Mix honey, sugar and hot water.
6. Mix the honey mixture, poppy seeds, and chopped nuts and wheat.
7. More honey can be added to taste.
8. Keep in refrigerator.

Ukrainian Dill Sauce

Ingredients:

2 tbsps. butter
2 tbsps. flour
1 cup fish stock or 1 cup chicken stock
1/2 cup light cream
1/2 tsp. salt
1 tbsp. finely chopped dill
1 lemon, juice of

Directions:

1. Melt butter and mix in flour, but do not let flour turn color.
2. Cook for 2 minutes or so.
3. Add stock and mix until smooth.
4. Cook several minutes, until thickened.
5. Remove from heat.
6. Mix in cream, salt, dill, and lemon juice.

Ukrainian Country Babka

Sponge Ingredients:

2 tsps. sugar
1/2 cup lukewarm water
2 (1/4 oz.) packages dry yeast
1 cup scalded milk, lukewarm
1 cup flour

Bread Ingredients:

6 eggs
1 tsp. salt
1 cup sugar
1 cup melted butter
2 tbsps. grated fresh lemon rind
5 1/2 cups sifted flour, about
1 cup raisins (or more)

Directions:

1. Dissolve the sugar in the lukewarm water, sprinkle the yeast over it, and let stand until softened.
2. For the sponge, combine dissolved yeast with the lukewarm milk and 1 cup of flour.
3. Beat well, cover, and allow the sponge to rise in a warm place until light and bubbly.
4. Beat the eggs with the salt, add the sugar gradually, and continue beating.
5. Beat in the butter and lemon rind.
6. Combine this mixture with the sponge.
7. Stir in the flour and knead in the bowl for about 10 minutes.
8. This dough should be slightly thicker than for the usual babka mixture.
9. Knead in the raisins.
10. Cover and let rise in a warm place until double in bulk.
11. Punch down, knead a few times, and let it rise again.
12. Butter tall, round baking pans (or coffee cans) with soft butter sprinkling them lightly with fine bread crumbs and fill them one-third full.
13. For this recipe you will need about 2 or 3 large coffee cans.
14. If you are going to use smaller cans, you will need more of them and use your judgment to how many you will need.
15. Adjust baking time for the smaller cans.
16. Cover and let rise in a warm place until the dough reaches the brim of the pan.

17. Brush the loaves with a beaten egg diluted with 2 Tbsps. of milk or water.
18. Bake in a moderately hot oven (400 degrees F) for about 15 minutes, then lower the temperature to 350 degrees F.
19. ,and continue baking for 40 minutes longer, or until done.
20. Avoid browning the top too deeply.
21. If necessary, cover with aluminum foil.
22. Remove the baked loaves from the oven and let them stand in the pans for 5 to 10 minutes.
23. Tip each loaf very gently from the pan onto a cloth-covered pillow.
24. Do not cool the loaves on a hard surface.
25. This is extremely important.
26. Careless handling of the baked babka may cause it to fall or settle.
27. As the loaves are cooling, change their position very gently a few times to prevent settling.
28. If desired, the cooled loaves may be iced or glazed and decorated with bakers' confetti.
29. This is the custom in the old country.
30. Babka is always sliced in rounds across the loaf.
31. The sliced bottom crust serves as a protective cover, and it is put back to prevent the loaf from drying.

Ukrainian Deep Fried Meatballs

Ingredients:

600 g. ground pork
400 g. ground beef
1 onion, grated
6 garlic cloves, minced
1 potato, grated
1 carrot, grated
1 mushroom, grated
2 tbsps. parsley, minced
2 tbsps. dill, minced
2 eggs
1/4 cup rice, cooked
1 tsp. salt
1 tsp. pepper
1/2 cup flour
1 cup oil

Directions:

1. Mix ground pork, ground beef, onion, garlic, potato, carrot, mushroom, parsley, dill, eggs, cooked rice, salt and pepper.(i used food processor for everything start with carrots add onion garlic potato herbs mushrooms meat then eggs but the rice ,fold in rice ,works great).
2. Make meatballs size of silver dollar.
3. Dust meatballs in flour.
4. Fry in hot oil 6 minutes until cooked.(the oil gets foamy).

Ukrainian Homemade Sausage (Kovbasa)

Ingredients:

5 lbs. pork shoulder
2 lbs. beef chuck
1 lb. pork fat
4-6 oz. coarse salt
2 tbsps. fresh ground black pepper
1 tbsp. allspice (ground)
1 head garlic
3 1/2 cups water
2 tsps. peperivka spiced whiskey, see below, to taste
3 yards natural hog casings (or as needed)

Directions:

1. Grind pork coarsely, once.
2. Bone and chill beef.
3. With a very sharp knife, dice 2 pounds beef into 1/4 inch cubes.
4. Dice 1/2 pound fat similarly and grind the other 1/2 pound of fat.
5. Mix meats and fat in a large bowl.
6. Mash peeled garlic with salt in a mortar, and add pepper and allspice.
7. Mix all ingredients.
8. Add 1 cup water for each 2 pounds of meat, then add whiskey.
9. Cook a small sample in a little boiling water.
10. Taste and adjust seasoning (be conservative with the salt).
11. Wash casing in cold water, rinsing several times.
12. Carefully thread 1 yard of casing over a sausage funnel and stuff, taking care not to leave air pockets.
13. Do not pack or sausages will burst while cooking.
14. Tie ends with string.
15. Repeat until all meat is used.
16. Refrigerate, loosely covered with towel, for 48 hours.
17. Sausage may be smoked (following smoker directions) or cooked fresh.
18. To cook fresh, simmer gently in a wide pot one-third full of water until cooked through, about 30-40 minutes.
19. Drain, cool, and refrigerate loosely covered.
20. To serve, sauté in a little fat for color.
21. Or serve cold in thin diagonal slices.

Ukrainian Tomato Salad

Ingredients:

2 sweet onions, chopped
2 tomatoes, chopped
3 green bell peppers, chopped
1 cup sour cream
1 tbsp. chopped fresh dill

Directions:

1. In a medium bowl, toss together sweet onions, tomatoes, and green bell peppers.
2. Blend sour cream and dill in a small bowl.
3. Lightly toss into the salad mixture.
4. Cover, and chill in the refrigerator until serving.

Ukrainian Cabbage Pie

Ingredients:

3 tbsps. butter
1 small head cabbage, finely chopped
3 hard-boiled eggs, peeled and chopped, or more to taste
3 sprigs fresh dill, finely chopped, or to taste
salt to taste
2 sheets yeasted puff pastry
1 egg, beaten

Directions:

1. Melt butter in a large skillet over medium-low heat.
2. Add cabbage and cook until softened but not browned, about 30 minutes.
3. Remove from heat and let cool, 10 to 15 minutes.
4. Preheat oven to 400 degrees F (200 degrees C).
5. Mix cooled cabbage with hard-boiled eggs and dill.
6. Season with salt.
7. Line a pie plate with 1 sheet of puff pastry.
8. Add cabbage filling, leaving some space around the edge.
9. Cover with the second sheet of puff pastry and pinch edges together. Glaze the top with beaten egg.
10. Bake in the preheated oven until golden brown, 40 to 45 minutes

Ukrainian Garden Salad

Ingredients:

10 romaine lettuce leaves, chopped
4 tomatoes, chopped
1 large cucumber, sliced
1 onion, sliced
1/2 cup fresh parsley, chopped
1 tbsp. salt
2 tbsps. lemon juice
1 tbsp. extra-virgin olive oil
1 cup sour cream

Directions:

1. Toss the romaine lettuce, tomatoes, cucumber, onion, and parsley together in a large bowl; season with salt. Drizzle the lemon juice and olive oil over the salad; stir.
2. Add the sour cream and mix until evenly coated.

Ukrainian Doughnuts

Ingredients:

1 cup all-purpose flour
2 eggs
1 tbsp. white sugar
1/2 tsp. vanilla extract, or to taste
1/4 tsp. salt
oil for frying
1 tbsp. confectioners' sugar, or to taste

Directions:

1. Mix farmer's cheese, flour, eggs, sugar, vanilla extract, and salt together in a bowl until a sticky dough forms.
2. Roll dough into 1-inch balls with wet hands to prevent sticking.
3. Heat oil in a deep-fryer or heavy saucepan to 375 degrees F (190 degrees C).
4. The oil should be hot but not smoking. It is ready for frying if you see little air bubbles around a wooden spoon placed in the oil.
5. Fry a batch of the dough balls in the hot oil until golden, about 2 minutes.
6. Place doughnuts on paper towels to soak up excess oil.
7. Repeat with remaining dough.
8. Sprinkle with confectioners' sugar.

Ukrainian Tea Cakes

Ingredients:

1 cup unsalted butter, room temperature
1 ⅓ cups confectioners' sugar, divided
1 cup finely chopped toasted walnuts
1/8 tsp. salt
1 tsp. vanilla extract
2 cups all-purpose flour
2 tbsps. all-purpose flour
1 cup confectioners' sugar for dusting, or more as needed

Directions:

1. Preheat oven to 350 degrees F (175 degrees C).
2. Arrange rack in center position of oven.
3. Place butter, 1/3 cup packed powdered sugar, walnuts, salt, and vanilla in a bowl.
4. Top with the flour.
5. Mix with your clean hands until the dough starts to clump up. Keep mixing by hand until all the flour and clumps of butter are evenly mixed into the dough and it can be easily formed into balls.
6. Scoop out dough and roll by hand into uniformly round balls, just slightly larger than 1 inch.
7. Place on a rimmed baking sheet lined with a silicone baking mat about 2 inches apart.
8. Bake in preheated oven until lightly golden, 15 to 25 minutes depending on the size of the cookies.
9. Let cool exactly 5 minutes then roll in remaining 1 cup confectioners' sugar. Let cookies cool completely and toss them again in the confectioners' sugar.

Ukrainian Poppy Seed Roll

Ingredients:

1 cup warm milk
2 (.25 oz.) packages active dry yeast
1 tsp. white sugar
1/2 cup white sugar
1/2 tsp. lemon zest
2 eggs
2 egg yolks
1/4 tsp. salt
6 cups all-purpose flour
7 tbsps. unsalted butter, melted

Filling Ingredients:

2 cups poppy seeds
1 cup milk, or as needed
1/2 cup raisins
2 egg whites
1/4 cup honey
1/4 cup white sugar
1/4 cup chopped walnuts
3 1/2 tbsps. unsalted butter, softened
1 egg
1 tbsp. water

Directions:

1. Combine warm milk, yeast, and 1 tsp. sugar in a large bowl; stir well. Let stand until yeast softens and begins to form a bubbly foam, about 5 minutes.
2. Stir 1/2 cup sugar and lemon zest into the yeast mixture.
3. Whisk in 2 eggs and egg yolks, 1 at time, mixing well after each addition.
4. Add salt.
5. Stir in flour gradually.
6. Add melted butter and blend well. Knead dough until glossy and elastic, about 10 minutes. Form into a ball and place in a large, lightly-oiled bowl and turn to coat.
7. Cover with a clean towel and let rise in a warm place until doubled in volume, about 1 hour.
8. Place poppy seeds in a small pot and cover with 1 cup milk or more as needed.
9. Bring to a simmer over medium heat.
10. Remove from heat and let sit, 15 to 20 minutes.

11. Drain milk. Pulse poppy seeds in a food processor, or leave them as is.
12. Add raisins, egg whites, honey, 1/4 cup sugar, walnuts, and 3 1/2 tbsps. butter to poppy seeds and stir to combine for the filling.
13. Punch down dough, turn out onto a lightly floured surface, and knead briefly.
14. Divide dough in half and roll one portion into a 10-inch sheet.
15. Cover with 1/2 the filling, leaving a 1/4- to 1/2-inch edge.
16. Roll up into a log.
17. Repeat with the second half.
18. Arrange both rolls onto a greased baking sheet.
19. Cover with a kitchen towel and let rise until doubled in volume, about 30 minutes more.
20. Preheat oven to 350 degrees F (175 degrees C).
21. Whisk remaining egg with 1 tbsp. water; brush mixture over tops of rolls.
22. Bake rolls in the preheated oven until golden, 20 to 25 minutes.

Ukrainian Ant Hill Cake

Dough Ingredients:

3/4 cup unsalted butter, melted
2 tbsps. unsalted butter, melted
1/2 cup white sugar
4 oz. sour cream
4 cups all-purpose flour
2 tsps. baking powder
Assembly:
3/4 cup unsalted butter, softened
2 tbsps. unsalted butter, softened
1 (13.4 oz.) can dulce de leche
2 tbsps. poppy seeds, for sprinkling

Directions:

1. Preheat oven to 350 degrees F (175 degrees C).
2. Grease a baking sheet.
3. Combine 3/4 cup plus 2 tbsps. of melted butter and sugar in a bowl; stir well.
4. Whisk in sour cream until smooth.
5. Mix flour and baking powder and sift over batter. Knead everything until a smooth, stiff dough forms.
6. Using the meat grinder attachment of your kitchen aid, pass handfuls of the dough through the grinder.
7. Spread ground dough pieces bits evenly over the prepared baking sheet.
8. Bake in the preheated oven until lightly browned, about 15 minutes.
9. Remove from the oven and allow to cool.
10. Beat 3/4 cup plus 2 tbsps. of softened butter in a bowl with an electric mixer until smooth and creamy.
11. Add dulce de leche and beat until well combined.
12. Add the cooled cake pieces to the caramel mixture and fold in with a spatula until well combined.
13. Mound the mixture onto a serving plate. Using buttered hands, form the mixture into an ant hill.
14. Sprinkle with poppy seeds.

Olivie - Ukrainian Potato Salad

Ingredients:

2 large potatoes, peeled and sliced lengthwise
3 carrots, peeled and sliced lengthwise
1 (15 oz.) can sweet peas, drained
3 dill pickles, chopped, or more to taste
1 onion, finely chopped
3 bologna slices, chopped (Optional)
2 hard-boiled eggs, chopped
2 tbsps. mayonnaise
2 tbsps. sour cream
1/2 tsp. salt
Ground black pepper to taste

Directions:

1. Place potatoes and carrots into a large pot and cover with salted water; bring to a boil.
2. Reduce heat to medium-low and simmer until tender, about 15 minutes.
3. Drain and rinse with cold water until cold. Dice potatoes and carrots.
4. Combine potatoes, carrots, sweet peas, pickles, onion, bologna, and eggs together in a large bowl.
5. Stir mayonnaise, sour cream, salt, and black pepper gently into potato mixture until well combined.
6. Cover bowl with plastic wrap and refrigerate until cold, at least 30 minutes.

Ukrainian Chicken and Pineapple Salad

Ingredients:

1 (10 oz.) can pineapple slices, drained and chopped (reserve a few slices for garnish)
1/2 pound skinless smoked chicken breast, cubed
1 cup grated mature Cheddar cheese
3/4 cup chopped walnuts
2 tbsps. sour cream
2 tbsps. mayonnaise
2 cloves garlic, minced (Optional)
salt and freshly ground black pepper to taste

Directions:

1. Combine cubed pineapple, chicken breast, Cheddar cheese, walnuts, sour cream, mayonnaise, and garlic in a bowl and mix well.
2. Season with salt and pepper. Spoon into a serving bowl and garnish with remaining pineapple rings.

Blini - Ukrainian Pancakes

Ingredients:

4 1/4 cups milk
5 eggs
⅓ tsp. salt
2 tbsps. white sugar
1/2 tsp. baking soda
1/8 tsp. citric acid powder
4 cups all-purpose flour
3 tbsps. vegetable oil
1 cup boiling water
⅔ cup butter, divided

Directions:

1. Beat together the milk and the eggs.
2. Stir in the salt and the sugar and mix well.
3. Add the baking soda and citric acid.
4. Blend in the flour.
5. Add the vegetable oil and pour in the boiling water, stirring constantly. The batter should be very thin, almost watery.
6. Set the bowl aside and let it rest for 20 minutes.
7. Melt a tbsp. of butter in a small frying pan over medium-high heat. Pick the pan up off the heat.
8. Pour in a ladleful of batter while you rotate your wrist, tilting the pan so the batter makes a circle and coats the bottom. The blini should be very thin.
9. Return the pan to the heat.
10. Cook the blini for 90 seconds.
11. Carefully lift up an edge of the blini to see if it's fully cooked: the edges will be golden and it should have brown spots on the surface. Flip the blini over and cook the other side for 1 minute.
12. Transfer the blini to a plate lined with a clean kitchen towel. Continue cooking the blini, adding an additional tbsp. of butter to the pan after each 4 blini. Stack them on top of each other and cover with the kitchen towel to keep warm.
13. Spread your favorite filling in the center of the blini, and fold three times to make a triangle shape. You can also fold up all 4 sides, like a small burrito.

Ukrainian Chicken and Pineapple Salad

Ingredients:

1 (10 oz.) can pineapple slices, drained and chopped (reserve a few slices for garnish)
1/2 pound skinless smoked chicken breast, cubed
1 cup grated mature Cheddar cheese
3/4 cup chopped walnuts
2 tbsps. sour cream
2 tbsps. mayonnaise
2 cloves garlic, minced (Optional)
Salt and freshly ground black pepper to taste

Directions:

1. Combine cubed pineapple, chicken breast, Cheddar cheese, walnuts, sour cream, mayonnaise, and garlic in a bowl and mix well.
2. Season with salt and pepper.
3. Spoon into a serving bowl and garnish with remaining pineapple rings.

Ukrainian Pork Roast

Ingredients:

2 1/4 pounds bone-in pork loin chops
3 tomatoes, sliced
2 onions, sliced
3/4 cup shredded Gouda cheese
1 clove garlic, crushed
salt and freshly ground black pepper
3 tbsps. prepared yellow mustard

Directions:

1. Preheat oven to 425 degrees F (220 degrees C).
2. Preheat oven to 350 degrees F (175 degrees C).
3. Cut pork into 1/4-inch slices lengthwise, stopping 1/2-inch from the bottom, so it can fan out like a book. Stuff tomatoes, onion, and Gouda cheese in between the slices.
4. Combine garlic and salt in a bowl, then stir in mustard and pepper.
5. Spread mixture all over the pork. Press pork slices firmly together and wrap in aluminum foil.
6. Bake in the preheated oven for about 1 hour 30 minutes.
7. Uncover and continue baking until nicely browned, about 30 minutes more.

Ukrainian Pelmeni

Dough Ingredients:

1 egg
1 tsp. vegetable oil
1 tsp. salt
3/4 cup warm water
3 cups all-purpose flour
1 tbsp. all-purpose flour

Filling Ingredients:

18 oz. ground beef
1 small onion, chopped
1 1/2 tbsps. ice-cold water
1 tbsp. coarse salt
Freshly ground pepper to taste

Directions:

1. Combine egg, vegetable oil, and salt in a measuring cup; add enough water to fill to 1 cup.
2. Pour into a bowl, add 3 cups flour, and knead into a smooth, elastic dough.
3. Cover with a kitchen towel and rest for 30 minutes.
4. Dust a baking sheet lightly with 1 tbsp. flour.
5. Combine ground beef, onion, water, salt, and pepper in a bowl and mix filling thoroughly by hand or using a fork.
6. Roll out a portion of the dough very thinly on a lightly floured surface and cut out 2 1/2-inch rounds with a cookie cutter or a wine glass. Keep the rest of the dough covered with a towel to avoid drying out.
7. Place 1/2 to 1 tsp. of filling on one side of the dough circle.
8. Fold dough over and seal the edges using fingers, forming a crescent. Join the ends and pinch them together.
9. Place on the prepared baking sheet.
10. Repeat with remaining dough and filling. Freeze pelmeni for 30 minutes to prevent them from sticking together.
11. Bring a large pot of lightly salted water to a simmer and drop small batches of frozen pelmeni into simmering water.
12. Cook and stir until the meat is cooked and pelmeni float to the top, about 5 minutes. Continue cooking for an additional 5 minutes. Transfer to serving plates using a slotted spoon.

Ukrainian Beet Salad with Herring

Ingredients:

3 whole russet potatoes
2 large carrots, peeled
2 beets, washed with tops and bottoms removed
1/2 yellow onion, chopped
1 (12 oz.) jar herring fillets, packed in oil
6 tbsps. mayonnaise
Salt and ground black pepper to taste

Directions:

1. Bring a large pot of water to a boil.
2. Cook the potatoes, carrots, and beets in the boiling water until cooked but still firm, 15 to 20 minutes for the potatoes, 25 to 30 minutes for the carrots, and 40 minutes for the beets. Allow each to cool to the touch before further handling.
3. Remove and discard the skins from the potatoes and beets. Shred the potatoes, carrots, and beets, keeping them separate.
4. Arrange about half the onion and half the herring fillets in a layer in the bottom of a bowl.
5. Cover the layer with about half of the grated potatoes, then a layer of about half the carrot, and finally about half the beet.
6. Spread about 3 tbsps. of mayonnaise over the salad; season with salt and pepper.
7. Repeat the layers in the same order to finish building the salad.
8. Cover with plastic wrap and chill in the refrigerator at least 1 hour.
9. Serve cold.

Solianka - Ukrainian Beef Soup

Ingredients:

2 oz. dried mushrooms
3/4 cup water
1/2 cup unsalted butter
3 onions, chopped
1 cup cooked diced veal
1 cup diced ham
1/4 pound kielbasa sausage, cut into 1 inch pieces
2 quarts beef stock
3 bay leaves
10 black peppercorns
2 dill pickles, diced
2 tbsps. capers
12 marinated mushrooms
1 (28 oz.) can Italian-style whole peeled tomatoes
2 tbsps. tomato paste
1 1/2 tbsps. all-purpose flour
12 kalamata olives
⅓ cup chopped fresh dill weed
1/4 tsp. dried marjoram
3 cloves garlic, minced
1/4 cup dill pickle juice
1 tsp. Hungarian sweet paprika
salt to taste
Ground black pepper to taste

Directions:

1. Soak mushrooms in 3/4 cup water until tender, 20 to 30 minutes.
2. Set aside.
3. Melt half the butter and sauté the onions, meats, and rehydrated mushrooms.
4. Add the stock and liquid from the mushrooms and bring to a boil.
5. Make a bouquet garni by tying the bay leaves and peppercorns tightly in cheesecloth. Lower the heat and add the bouquet garni, pickles, capers, and marinated mushrooms. Simmer 10-15 minutes.
6. Melt remaining butter in a skillet and cook the tomatoes and tomato paste for a few minutes, then add the flour and sauté for another few minutes.
7. Add a cup of the soup to the skillet and stir in well, then return pan ingredients to the soup pot.

8. Add the olives, dill, marjoram, garlic, pickle juice, and paprika. Adjust soup's seasoning with salt and pepper; simmer another 10-15 minutes.
9. Remove pot from heat and remove bouquet garni. Adjust seasonings and serve with sour cream and lemon.

Ukrainian Beet and Potato Salad

Ingredients:

2 beets
4 small potatoes
2 small carrots
3 small dill pickles, diced
1/4 cup vegetable oil
2 tbsps. champagne vinegar
salt to taste
3 green onions, chopped

Directions:

1. Bring a large pot of water to a boil, and cook beets until tender, about 30 minutes.
2. Bring a separate pot of water to a boil and cook potatoes and carrots until tender, about 20 minutes.
3. Drain vegetables, cool, and remove skins. Dice and place in a large bowl.
4. Place the diced pickles in the bowl with beets, potatoes, and carrots. Drizzle the olive oil and vinegar over the mixture and toss to coat.
5. Season with salt.
6. Sprinkle with green onions. Chill completely before serving.

Ukrainian Tomato Salad

Ingredients:

2 sweet onions, chopped
2 tomatoes, chopped
3 green bell peppers, chopped
1 cup sour cream
1 tbsp. chopped fresh dill

Directions:

1. In a medium bowl, toss together sweet onions, tomatoes, and green bell peppers.
2. Blend sour cream and dill in a small bowl.
3. Lightly toss into the salad mixture.
4. Cover, and chill in the refrigerator until serving.

Ukrainian Black Bread

Ingredients:

1 1/2 cups water
2 tbsps. cider vinegar
2 1/2 cups bread flour
1 cup rye flour
1 tsp. salt
2 tbsps. margarine
2 tbsps. dark corn syrup
1 tbsp. brown sugar
3 tbsps. unsweetened cocoa powder
1 tsp. instant coffee granules
1 tbsp. caraway seed
1/4 tsp. fennel seed (Optional)
2 tsps. active dry yeast

Directions:

1. Place ingredients into the bread machine in order suggested by the manufacturer.
2. Use the whole wheat, regular crust setting.
3. After the baking cycle ends, remove bread from pan, place on a cake rack, and allow to cool for 1 hour before slicing.

Ukrainian Deviled Eggs

Ingredients:

1 small beet, peeled
2 tbsps. mayonnaise
2 tsps. Dijon mustard
2 tsps. sweet pickle relish (Optional)
6 eggs
1 pinch ground paprika, or to taste
salt and ground black pepper to taste
12 sprigs fresh cilantro (Optional)

Directions:

1. Place beet in a small saucepan with water to cover; bring to a simmer and cook until tender, about 15 minutes.
2. Drain and cool. Grate beet on medium holes of a grater.
3. Place grated beet in a bowl; stir in mayonnaise, mustard, and relish.
4. Place eggs in a saucepan; cover with water.
5. Bring to a boil, remove from heat, and let eggs stand in hot water for 15 minutes.
6. Remove eggs from hot water, cool under cold running water, and peel.
7. Cut each egg in half lengthwise; place egg yolks in a bowl.
8. Mash egg yolks with a fork; stir beet mixture into egg yolks.
9. Season with paprika, salt, and pepper.
10. Place egg whites cut-side up on a serving platter. Spoon yolk mixture into egg white halves; top with cilantro.

Kotlety - Ukrainian Burgers

Ingredients:

1 small onion, grated
1 clove garlic, minced
1 large egg, lightly beaten
salt and ground black pepper to taste
1 cup water, or more as needed
1 cup bread crumbs, or as needed
3 tbsps. vegetable oil, or to taste

Directions:

1. Combine pork, onion, garlic, and egg in a large bowl.
2. Season with salt and pepper.
3. Add water a little at a time, stirring until pork mixture absorbs it and reaches the consistency of sour cream.
4. Pour bread crumbs onto a plate. Scoop up medium-sized balls of the pork mixture with a tbsp. and drop into the bread crumbs; flip to coat both sides.
5. Heat oil in a frying pan over medium heat.
6. Fry patties, in batches if necessary, until golden brown, 5 to 6 minutes per side.

Kulich (Ukrainian Easter Cake)

Ingredients:

1 cup golden raisins
1 tbsp. vodka
1 tsp. white sugar
1/4 cup lukewarm water
1 (.25 oz.) package active dry yeast
1 cup milk
1 pinch saffron threads
1 tsp. ground cardamom
1/2 cup white sugar
1 cup all-purpose flour
1/2 cup butter, melted
1/2 cup white sugar
1/4 cup orange blossom honey
1 lemon, zested
2 tsps. vanilla extract
1 pinch salt
2 eggs
1 egg yolk
3 cups all-purpose flour, divided
1/2 cup sliced almonds
4 clean 14-oz. food cans
1 egg white
1 1/2 cups confectioners' sugar, or more as needed
1/2 tsp. lemon juice
2 tbsps. toasted sliced almonds, or as needed

Directions:

1. Place golden raisins into a bowl, drizzle with vodka, and allow raisins to soften overnight.
2. Mix 1 tsp. sugar into lukewarm water in a bowl until sugar dissolves.
3. Stir yeast into the water and let stand until the yeast mixture is frothy, about 10 minutes.
4. Heat milk in a saucepan over medium-low heat until very warm but not simmering.
5. Stir in saffron threads and cardamom, remove from heat, and let the milk mixture stand until lukewarm.
6. Transfer yeast mixture into a large mixing bowl.
7. Stir milk mixture, 1/2 cup sugar, and 1 cup flour into the yeast mixture, beating until the batter is smooth.
8. Cover the bowl with plastic wrap and allow to rise in a warm place for 1 hour.

9. Mix melted butter, 1/2 cup sugar, orange blossom honey, lemon zest, vanilla extract, and salt together in a bowl. Beat butter mixture into the batter, then beat in eggs and egg yolk.
10. Mix 2 1/2 cups of flour into the dough.
11. Sprinkle remaining 1/2 cup flour onto a work surface and knead dough until it holds together, about 5 minutes; knead soaked golden raisins and 1/2 cup almonds into the dough until well distributed.
12. Form dough into a ball and place into an oiled bowl; turn dough around in the bowl several times to coat outside of dough.
13. Cover bowl with plastic wrap and allow to rise in a warm place until doubled, about 1 1/2 hours.
14. Punch down dough, knead a few times, and divide dough into 4 pieces. Coat inside of clean 14-oz. cans with butter. Line cans with parchment paper.
15. Roll each piece of dough into a ball, place into a can, and press dough lightly against the inside bottom of can.
16. Cover cans with a cloth and allow dough to rise to the top of the cans, about 45 minutes.
17. Preheat oven to 350 degrees F (175 degrees C).
18. Place a baking sheet into the oven; place the cans of dough upright into oven on baking sheet.
19. Bake until kulich are risen and lightly browned, 45 to 50 minutes.
20. Let kulich cool in the cans for about 15 minutes before gently removing from cans to finish cooling on racks.
21. Beat egg white in a bowl with an electric mixer on medium speed until frothy; beat in confectioners' sugar until the mixture holds stiff peaks. Beat lemon juice into frosting.
22. Frost the tops of the kulich and sprinkle tops with 2 tbsps. toasted sliced almonds. Refrigerate leftovers.

Ukrainian Beef Stroganoff

Ingredients:

2 tbsps. all-purpose flour
1 pound sirloin steak, pounded to 1/4-inch thickness and cut into thin strips across the grain
2 tbsps. vegetable oil
2 tbsps. sour cream
1 tbsp. tomato paste
salt and freshly ground black pepper to taste
1 tbsp. water, or as needed (Optional)

Directions:

1. Place flour in a bowl.
2. Toss beef strips in flour until coated on all sides.
3. Heat oil in a large skillet over medium-high heat. Sauté streak strips in the hot oil until browned, 3 to 5 minutes.
4. Add sour cream, tomato paste, salt, and pepper; stir to combine.
5. Add some water if mixture is too thick.
6. Cover and simmer over low heat until meat is cooked through and soft, 20 to 25 minutes.

Ukrainian Pirozhki

Ingredients:

1 tbsp. white sugar
1 tbsp. active dry yeast
2 tbsps. butter, melted
1 egg
1 tsp. salt
6 cups all-purpose flour
1 tbsp. butter
1/2 medium head cabbage, finely chopped
6 hard-cooked eggs, chopped
Salt and pepper to taste

Directions:

1. Place 1/2 cup milk in a cup or small bowl.
2. Stir in sugar and sprinkle yeast over the top.
3. Set aside until foamy, about 10 minutes.
4. Pour the remaining milk into a large bowl.
5. Add the melted butter, egg, salt and 1 cup of flour to the large bowl with the milk.
6. Stir in the yeast mixture.
7. Mix in flour 1 cup at a time until dough pulls away from the sides of the bowl and doesn't stick to your hands.
8. Cover the bowl loosely and set in a warm place to rise for about 1 hour. Dough should almost triple in size.
9. While you wait for the dough to rise, melt the remaining butter in a large skillet over medium heat.
10. Add cabbage and cook, stirring frequently, until cabbage has wilted.
11. Mix in the eggs and season with salt and pepper. Continue to cook, stirring occasionally until cabbage is tender.
12. Set this aside for the filling.
13. Place the risen dough onto a floured surface and gently form into a long snake about 2 inches wide.
14. Cut into 1 inch pieces and roll each piece into a ball. Flatten the balls by hand until they are 4 to 5 inches across.
15. Place a spoonful of the cabbage filling in the center and fold in half to enclose. Pinch the edges together to seal in the filling.
16. Preheat the oven to 400 degrees F (200 degrees C). Line one or two baking sheets with aluminum foil.
17. Place the pirozhki onto the baking sheet, leaving room between them for them to grow.
18. Bake for 20 minutes in the preheated oven, or until golden brown.

Ukrainian Salmon and Potato Salad

Ingredients:

2 eggs
3 medium baking potatoes, peeled and cubed
1 tbsp. olive oil
1 large onion, chopped
1 (16 oz.) can salmon, drained
1 cup mayonnaise, or as needed
1 tbsp. chopped fresh parsley, for garnish

Directions:

1. Place eggs in a saucepan and cover with cold water.
2. Bring water to a boil and immediately remove from heat.
3. Cover and let eggs stand in hot water for 10 to 12 minutes.
4. Remove from hot water, cool, and peel.
5. While the eggs are cooking, place the potatoes in a saucepan with just enough water to cover.
6. Bring to a boil, and cook for 10 to 15 minutes, or until tender.
7. Remove from heat, drain, and set aside.
8. Heat oil in a skillet over medium heat.
9. Add onions, and sauté until lightly browned and translucent, about 10 minutes.
10. Flake salmon and spread it over the bottom of a glass baking dish or serving dish.
11. Spread the sautéed onions over the salmon.
12. Gently spread a little bit of the mayonnaise over the onion layer.
13. Top with potatoes, and spread enough mayonnaise just to add moisture to the layer. Finally, slice the eggs, and cover the layer of potatoes.
14. Spread mayonnaise over the eggs, and garnish with chopped parsley. If you wish, you can reserve some of the egg to chop and sprinkle over the top as well. Chill for 1 hour before serving.

German Ukrainian-Dakota Knefla

Ingredients:

2 cups all-purpose flour
1 tsp. baking powder
1 tsp. salt
1/4 tsp. black pepper
1 egg
1/4 cup milk
2 tbsps. vegetable oil
3 potatoes, peeled and diced

Directions:

1. Whisk the flour, baking powder, salt, and pepper together in a bowl.
2. Whisk together the egg and milk in a separate bowl; stir in the flour mixture until a smooth dough is formed.
3. Fill a large pot with lightly salted water and bring to a rolling boil over high heat. Once the water is boiling, cut the dough into bite sized pieces with scissors into the boiling water. Boil for 20 minutes; drain well.
4. Heat the oil in a large skillet over medium-low heat; add the knefla and potatoes.
5. Stirring occasionally, cook until the potatoes are tender and the knefla are golden brown, about 20 minutes.

Kholdnyk - Ukrainian Cold Beet Soup

Ingredients:

4 cups fat-free buttermilk
1 cucumber - peeled, seeded, quartered lengthwise and diced
1 (15 oz.) can sliced beets with liquid
3 green onions, chopped
2 tbsps. chopped fresh dill
1/2 tsp. salt, or to taste
2 tbsps. white vinegar, or to taste

Directions:

1. Mix the buttermilk, cucumber, beets with their juice, green onions, dill, salt, and vinegar in a bowl; stir to mix thoroughly, and chill, covered, in refrigerator at least 2 hours or overnight for best flavor.
2. Serve cold.

Ukrainian Layered Cake

Ingredients:

1 1/2 cups white sugar
3 eggs
1 1/2 cups all-purpose flour
1 1/2 tsps. baking soda
1 ⅓ cups sour cream
1/2 cup chopped walnuts
⅓ cup raisins
1/2 cup poppy seeds
3/4 cup unsalted butter, softened
2 tbsps. unsalted butter, softened
1 (14.5 oz.) can sweetened condensed milk

Directions:

1. Preheat oven to 350 degrees F (175 degrees C).
2. Grease and flour three 9-inch round cake pans.
3. Beat sugar and eggs together in a bowl using an electric mixer for 5 minutes.
4. Sift flour and baking soda together in another bowl. Beat into the egg and sugar mixture gradually, alternating with sour cream, until a smooth batter forms.
5. Divide batter equally between 3 bowls.
6. Fold walnuts into the first bowl, raisins into the second bowl, and poppy seeds to the third.
7. Pour each bowl into its own separate cake pan.
8. Bake cakes in the preheated oven until a toothpick inserted into the centers comes out clean, 20 to 30 minutes.
9. Let cakes cool in pans for a few minutes.
10. Remove from pans carefully; let cool completely, at least 30 minutes.
11. Beat 3/4 cup plus 2 tbsps. butter in a bowl using an electric mixer until creamy.
12. Add condensed milk slowly, mixing with a fork or spatula in a clockwise motion.
13. Spread a couple of tbsps. of buttercream onto a large cake plate.
14. Place one of the cakes onto the butter cream on the cake plate.
15. Spread another few tbsps. buttercream over the cake and lay another cake on top.
16. Repeat with the remaining cake and cover top and sides with remaining buttercream. Decorate as desired.

Syrniki - Ukrainian Cheese Pancakes

Ingredients:

3 tbsps. white sugar
1 cup quark, well drained
5 tbsps. all-purpose flour, plus extra for dusting
1 1/2 tsps. vanilla sugar (Optional)
1/4 tsp. salt
Oil for frying

Directions:

1. Beat egg and white sugar together in a bowl until smooth.
2. Whisk in quark cheese, flour, vanilla sugar, and salt.
3. Mix well until dough is thick and sticky.
4. Divide dough into 5 to 6 portions. Form into balls and coat with some flour. Flatten slightly to form into discs (syrniki).
5. Heat oil in skillet over medium-low heat.
6. Add the syrniki; fry until browned, 5 minutes per side.

Ukrainian Salad 'Olive'

Ingredients:

6 potatoes, peeled
1 carrot, or more to taste
4 eggs
6 large pickles, cut into cubes
1 (15 oz.) can peas, drained
1/2 cup cubed fully cooked ham, or to taste
1 tbsp. chopped fresh parsley, or to taste (Optional)
1/2 cup mayonnaise, or to taste

Directions:

1. Bring a large pot of water to a boil; add potatoes and carrot. Return mixture to a boil and add eggs; cook until potatoes are tender, 20 to 30 minutes.
2. Drain and slightly cool mixture. Chop potatoes and carrot; peel and chop eggs.
3. Mix potatoes, carrot, eggs, pickles, peas, ham, and parsley together in a large bowl; stir in mayonnaise until salad is evenly coated.

Ukrainian Rice and Crab Salad

Ingredients:

1 cup water
1/2 cup uncooked white rice
1 (15.25 oz.) can whole kernel corn, drained
1 cup imitation crabmeat, flaked
4 hard-boiled eggs, mashed
1 onion, minced
4 cornichons, minced
1 pinch salt and ground black pepper to taste
3 tbsps. mayonnaise
1 clove garlic, finely chopped
1 bunch fresh dill, chopped

Directions:

1. Bring water and rice to a boil in a saucepan.
2. Reduce heat to medium-low, cover, and simmer until rice is tender and water has been absorbed, 20 to 25 minutes.
3. Remove from heat and cool for a minimum of 4 hours or overnight.
4. Combine cooked and cooled rice, corn, imitation crab, eggs, onion, and cornichons in a bowl.
5. Season with salt and pepper.
6. Stir together mayonnaise and garlic in a small bowl; pour over salad.
7. Mix well.
8. Sprinkle with chopped dill.

Ukrainian Sour Cream Cake

Cake Ingredients:

3 eggs
1 cup white sugar
1 cup all-purpose flour
2 tbsps. all-purpose flour

Filling Ingredients:

1 3/4 cups sour cream
1 cup white sugar
1 tsp. lemon juice (Optional)

Directions:

1. Preheat oven to 325 degrees F (165 degrees C).
2. Grease a 9-inch springform pan.
3. Combine eggs and 1 cup sugar in a large bowl; beat with an electric mixer for 5 minutes until mixture is smooth and thick. Sift 1 cup plus 2 tbsps. flour on top and carefully mix into the batter using a wooden spoon or a spatula.
4. Pour batter into the prepared springform pan.
5. Bake in the preheated oven until a toothpick inserted into the middle of the cake comes out clean, 25 to 30 minutes. Allow to cool in the pan for 10 minutes.
6. Remove from pan and allow to completely cool on a wire rack, about 1 hour.
7. Combine sour cream, 1 cup sugar, and lemon juice in a large bowl; beat with an electric mixer for 10 to 15 minutes until a thick cream forms.
8. Cut cake horizontally into 3 layers.
9. Place bottom layer on a cake platter and spread with a layer of cream filling.
10. Add second layer and spread another layer of filling on top. Finish cake by placing the third layer on top and cover cake from all sides with the remaining cream.
11. Cover and refrigerate until serving.

Ukrainian Eggnog

Ingredients:

1/2 (1.5 fluid oz.) jigger spiced rum
1 (1.5 fluid oz.) jigger coffee flavored liqueur
3/4 cup eggnog
1 pinch ground nutmeg

Directions:

1. Pour the spiced rum and coffee liqueur into a glass.
2. Top with eggnog.
3. Stir and sprinkle some nutmeg on the top.

Ukrainian Mushroom Bake

Ingredients:

4 tbsps. vegetable oil, divided
7 cups quartered button mushrooms
1 cup sour cream
1 onion, chopped
salt and ground black pepper to taste
1 1/4 cups shredded Gouda cheese

Directions:

1. Preheat the oven to 425 degrees F (220 degrees C).
2. Heat 2 tbsps. oil in a skillet over medium heat. Increase heat to high and add mushrooms.
3. Cook and stir until golden brown, 6 to 8 minutes.
4. Do not cook so long so that they begin to release a lot of liquid.
5. Add sour cream, mix well, and transfer mixture to a casserole dish.
6. Heat remaining 2 tbsps. oil in a second skillet over medium heat and cook onion until soft and translucent, 4 to 6 minutes.
7. Distribute onions over mushrooms and season with salt and pepper.
8. Sprinkle with Gouda cheese.
9. Bake in the preheated oven until the cheese has melted and is golden brown, 15 to 20 minutes.

Shchi - Ukrainian Cabbage Soup

Ingredients:

3 tbsps. butter
1 large onion chopped
1 large head cabbage, cut into shreds
1 large carrot, peeled and coarsely grated
1 rib celery, chopped
1 bay leaf
Black peppercorns, to taste
8 cups water, or vegetable stock
2 large russet potatoes, peeled and coarsely chopped
2 large tomatoes (peeled, seeded, and chopped; or a 14-oz. can of undrained diced tomatoes)
Salt to taste
Pepper to taste
Garnish: sour cream
Garnish: fresh dill

Directions:

1. Gather the ingredients.
2. Add the butter to a large saucepan or Dutch oven over medium heat.
3. Add the onion and sauté until translucent.
4. Add the shredded cabbage, grated carrot, and chopped celery. Sauté about 3 minutes, stirring frequently.
5. Add the bay leaf and black peppercorns.
6. Pour in the water or vegetable stock and bring to a boil.
7. Reduce the heat and simmer, covered, for 15 minutes.
8. Add the potatoes to the soup and bring it back to a boil.
9. Reduce the heat and simmer, covered, until the potatoes are tender, about 10 minutes.
10. Add the chopped fresh tomatoes (or undrained canned tomatoes) and bring the soup back to a boil.
11. Reduce the heat and simmer, uncovered, for 5 minutes.
12. Season with salt and pepper to taste.
13. Remove the bay leaf and peppercorns from the pot (some cooks leave the peppercorns in).
14. Serve bowls of the soup topped with fresh sour cream and fresh dill and enjoy.

Borscht

Ingredients:

3 pounds bone-in beef shank
2 tbsps. vegetable oil
1 onion, chopped
6 cups water
1/2 pounds carrots, cut into 1 inch pieces
2 stalks celery, cut into 1 inch pieces
⅓ medium head cabbage, shredded
1 pounds beets, peeled and shredded
1 cup tomato juice
1 tbsp. lemon juice
2 tsps. white sugar
2 tsps. salt
1/8 tsp. ground black pepper

Directions:

1. In a large pot over medium heat, brown beef in oil.
2. Stir in onion and water, reduce heat and simmer, covered, 2 hours, until meat is tender.
3. Remove meat from broth and set aside to cool slightly.
4. Stir carrots, celery, cabbage, beets, tomato juice, lemon juice, sugar, salt and pepper into broth.
5. When meat is cool enough to handle, cut meat from bone and into bite-size pieces and return to soup.
6. Simmer until vegetables are tender, 20 to 30 minutes.

Ukrainian Borscht

Ingredients:

2 small beets, peeled and coarsely grated
3 tbsps. vinegar
2 tbsps. vegetable oil, or as needed
1 onion, chopped
2 carrots, coarsely grated
8 cups water
1/4 medium head cabbage, shredded
3/4 cup dry yellow lentils
3 medium potatoes, peeled and diced
salt and pepper to taste
2 tbsps. tomato paste
2 tbsps. sour cream, or more to taste
2 tbsps. chopped fresh dill

Directions:

1. Combine beets and vinegar in a small frying pan over low heat.
2. Cook, while stirring, until soft, about 15 minutes.
3. Heat oil in a large frying pan over low heat while beets are cooking.
4. Add onion and stir for 2 minutes.
5. Add carrots and cook, stirring occasionally, until soft, about 10 minutes.
6. Set aside.
7. In the meantime, bring water to a simmer in a large saucepan.
8. Add cabbage and lentils.
9. Cook for 10 minutes.
10. Add potatoes and cook for 10 minutes more.
11. Stir in cooked beets and onion-carrot mixture.
12. Season with salt and pepper.
13. Add tomato paste and simmer until all vegetables are tender, about 10 minutes more.
14. Serve with sour cream and dill.

Easter White Borscht

Ingredients:

9 cups water
3 pounds kielbasa sausage
2 cloves garlic, whole
3 tbsps. butter
2 leeks, chopped
1 white onion, diced
3 cloves garlic, minced
2 bay leaves
1 1/2 cups sour cream
1/4 cup all-purpose flour, or more as needed
1/4 cup chopped fresh dill
2 tbsps. white vinegar, or more to taste
salt and ground black pepper to taste
4 hard-cooked eggs, chopped

Directions:

1. Bring water, kielbasa, and 2 whole cloves garlic to boil in a large pot; reduce heat to medium and simmer for 30 minutes.
2. Remove sausage and pour liquid into a separate bowl.
3. Cut sausage into cubes.
4. Melt butter over medium heat in the pot used to boil sausage; cook and stir leeks, onion, and minced garlic until vegetables are tender, about 5 minutes. Transfer vegetables to a blender; add about 1/2 cup reserved sausage water and blend until smooth, adding more water as needed.
5. Pour vegetable puree and remaining sausage water back into the original pot.
6. Add bay leaves and bring borscht to a simmer over medium heat; remove and discard leaves.
7. Whisk sour cream and flour in a bowl until smooth; gradually whisk into borscht until thickened.
8. Stir dill and vinegar into soup and season with salt and black pepper.
9. Divide cubed sausage and chopped eggs into bowls; ladle borscht over sausage and egg.

Ukha - Ukrainian Fish Soup

Ingredients:

2 Tbsp. olive oil
1 medium onion, thinly sliced
2 medium carrots, thinly sliced
4 cups fish stock (or vegetable stock)
4 cups water
3-4 medium potatoes, peeled and cubed
3 bay leaves
10 black peppercorns
Salt, to taste
1/3 cup millet *
1/2 pound fresh cod filet, ** cut into cubes
1/2 pound salmon filet, ** cut into cubes
Handful fresh dill and/or parsley (for serving)

Directions:

1. In a medium pot, heat the olive oil over medium-high heat.
2. Add the onions and cook, stirring occasionally until the onions start to caramelize.
3. Add the carrots and cook until the carrots start to soften, about 4 more minutes.
4. Add the stock, water, potatoes, bay leaves, and black peppercorns.
5. Season with salt and bring to a boil.
6. Reduce heat, cover and cook for 10 minutes.
7. Add the millet and cook for 15 more minutes until millet and potatoes are cooked.
8. Gently add the fish cubes.
9. Stir and bring the soup to a simmer. The fish will cook through very fast, so make sure to not overcook them. They are done when the flesh is opaque and flakes easily.
10. Garnish the soup with chopped fresh dill or parsley before serving.

Stuffed Cabbage Rolls

Filling Ingredients:

1/2 lb. lean ground pork
1/2 lb. ground chicken breast
1 cup half-cooked rice
1/2 onion, minced
1 clove garlic, minced
1/2 red bell pepper, finely chopped
1 small carrot, grated
2 tbsps. butter
1 egg, beaten
1/2 tsp. salt
1/4 tsp. pepper

Cabbage Rolls Ingredients:

1 head of green cabbage
2 tbsps. tomato paste
2 bay leaves
3 whole peppercorns
1 large carrot , chopped
1-2 tbsps. sour cream
Salt , to taste
Water
1 tbsp. butter
1 heaping tbsp. all-purpose flour
Fresh dill (optional), for garnish

Directions:

1. With a sharp knife, remove the core from cabbage.
2. Place cabbage, core side down, in a large pot with about 2-3 inches of boiling salted water, cover and cook on low for 5 minutes.
3. Remove from heat and carefully turn the cabbage cut side up.
4. Next, using tongs, remove the cabbage leaves and set them aside to cool a bit. You will need about 10 leaves.
5. Coarsely chop the remaining cabbage and place it over the bottom of a large pot or Dutch oven (optional).
6. Set aside.
7. Using a knife, cut away the thick center stem from the outside of each leaf (see photo above), without cutting all the way through.
8. Heat the butter in a large pan over medium heat until melted.
9. Add the onion, garlic, bell pepper, and carrot and sauté, stirring frequently, for 5 minutes or until soften.
10. Remove from heat and let cool.

11. In a large bowl, combine the pork, chicken, rice, egg, sautéed onion mixture, salt, and pepper.
12. Place 1/4 to 1/2 cup of meat on each cabbage leaf near stem end.
13. Fold over each side and tightly roll the cabbage roll. At this point, cabbage rolls can be frozen until ready to use.
14. Once you have made all your rolls, place them (with the end of the leaf face down) on top of the chopped cabbage in the pot.
15. Add peppercorns, chopped carrot and bay leaves.
16. In a small bowl, combine tomato paste with 1 cup of water and pour over rolls.
17. Add enough water so the rolls are almost covered.
18. Add salt to taste.
19. Cover the pot and bring to a boil over medium-high heat.
20. Reduce heat and simmer, covered, for 50-60 minutes, or until the filling inside the cabbage is cooked through.
21. For the sauce: Remove the cabbage rolls from the pot.
22. Melt 1 tbsp. of butter in the microwave and mix it with flour.
23. Add this mixture to the pot, stir gently and boil for a few minutes. Take off the heat and stir in the sour cream.
24. Serve the cabbage rolls topped with the sauce and accompanied by boiled or mashed potatoes. Garnish with fresh dill, if desired. Enjoy!

Plov - Ukrainian Lamb Pilaf

Ingredients:

2 oz. raisins
4 oz. pitted prunes
1 tbsp. fresh lemon juice
1 oz. butter
1 large onion, chopped
1 pound boneless lamb, trimmed and cut into cubes
8 oz. lean ground lamb
2 garlic cloves, crushed
2 1/2 cups lamb stock or vegetable stock
2 cups long-grain white rice, rinsed and drained
Large pinch saffron
Salt and pepper, to taste
Garnish: flat-leaf parsley

Directions:

1. Place the raisins and prunes into a small bowl and pour over enough water to cover.
2. Add lemon juice and let soak for at least 1 hour.
3. Drain. Roughly chop the prunes.
4. Meanwhile, heat the butter in a large pan, add the onion, and cook for 5 minutes.
5. Add cubed lamb, ground lamb, and crushed garlic cloves.
6. Fry for 5 minutes, stirring constantly until browned.
7. Pour 2/3 cup of stock into the pan.
8. Bring to a boil, then lower the heat, cover, and simmer for 1 hour, or until the lamb is tender.
9. Add the remaining stock and bring to a boil.
10. Add rinsed long-grain white rice and a large pinch of saffron.
11. Stir, then cover, and simmer for 15 minutes, or until the rice is tender.
12. Add the drained raisins, drained chopped prunes, and salt and pepper to taste.
13. Heat through for a few minutes, then turn out onto a warmed serving dish and garnish with sprigs of flat-leaf parsley.

Carrot Salad

Ingredients:

4 medium/large carrots, cut into match sticks
1 Tbsp white vinegar (5%)
1 garlic clove, pressed (add more if you like)
1 tsp coriander seeds, crushed
1/2 tsp salt
1/2 tsp sugar
1/4 tsp freshly ground black pepper
2 Tbsp oil (olive or canola)
1 medium onion, finely diced

Directions:

1. Julianne carrots and dice onions.
2. Mix together carrots, vinegar, garlic, coriander, salt and sugar.
3. Heat oil in the medium skillet over medium/high heat than sauté onion until soft and golden (about 5-6 minutes).
4. Add pepper and stir the onions and pepper quickly. Immediately after stirring, add the onion to the carrots.
5. Mix everything well and let salad sit for at least 1 hour before serving.
6. Add more salt & sugar (in equal parts), to taste.
7. If it's too flavorful after 1 hour, add more carrot.
8. Serve as a side dish. Enjoy

Kurnik: Ukrainian Chicken Pie

Cream Cheese Pastry Ingredients:

4 oz. butter, cold, cut into chunks
4 oz. cream cheese, cold, cut into chunks
1 cup all-purpose flour

Pie Filling Ingredients:

2 cups water or chicken broth
1 cup rice (rinsed)
2 large onions, thinly sliced
8 oz. mushrooms, sliced
2 tbsps. butter
1 cup half-and-half
1 tbsp. cornstarch
1 cup chicken broth
3 cups cooked chicken meat (diced)
2 tbsps. parsley (chopped)
1 tsp. salt
Black pepper (to taste)
4 hard-cooked eggs (finely chopped)
1 tbsp. dill (chopped)

Directions:

Egg Wash Ingredients:

1 egg yolk
1 tbsp. water (beaten)

Pastry Directions:

1. Using the steel blade of a food processor, place all ingredients into the work bowl.
2. Process until dough forms a ball, 18 to 20 seconds. Chilling isn't necessary.
3. When ready, roll on a lightly floured surface to the measurements of the pan you are going to cover plus about 2 inches on each side. An ungreased 12x7-inch baking dish works well for this recipe.

Filling Directions:

1. Bring 2 cups water or chicken broth to a boil in a medium saucepan. If using water, add salt.
2. Stir in rinsed and drained rice. Return to a boil, reduce heat, cover and simmer for 15 minutes or until all the liquid has been absorbed and rice is tender.

3. Uncover, fluff with a fork and remove from heat.
4. Meanwhile, melt 2 tbsps. butter in a large skillet.
5. Add onions and mushrooms, and sauté until onions are tender and somewhat caramelized.
6. Stir cornstarch into half-and-half and add to onions along with 1 cup chicken broth, bring to a boil, stirring constantly.
7. Reduce heat and simmer 1 minute.
8. Add chicken, parsley, salt, and pepper and mix thoroughly.
9. Remove from heat.
10. In a medium bowl, mix the hard-cooked eggs with the dill, and set aside.
11. Heat oven to 400 degrees F.
12. Spread 1/3 of the cooked rice into the bottom of the ungreased pan then layer 1/2 of the chicken mixture and 1/2 of the egg-dill mixture.
13. Spread on another 1/3 of the rice, the rest of the chicken mixture and the rest of the egg-dill mixture.
14. Spread on the remaining rice.
15. Place rolled-out pastry crust on top. Turn the edges of overhanging pastry to the inside. Brush pastry completely with egg-water wash.
16. Using the back of a fork, make decorative crisscross marks all over.
17. Cut a slit in the center for an air vent. Alternatively, you can make fancy leaves or bird shapes out of leftover pastry dough to decorate the top.
18. Place dish on a baking sheet to catch any drips, and bake 30 minutes or until golden and bubbly.
19. Remove from oven and let rest 10 minutes.
20. Serve hot.

Ukrainian Peas

Ingredients:

1/2 cup dried whole peas
4 cups cold water
3 tbsps. butter
1 tsp. salt
1 tsp. white sugar
1 tbsp. dried parsley (Optional)
1 tsp. all-purpose flour, or as needed (Optional)

Directions:

1. Place peas with cold water in a pot; leave to soak for 24 to 48 hours.
2. Bring peas to a boil in the soaking water.
3. Reduce heat to low and simmer until peas are very soft, stirring occasionally, about 1 1/2 hours, adding water if needed.
4. Stir butter, salt, sugar, and parsley into peas. For thicker peas, add flour and cook and stir until thick, about 5 minutes.

Pelmeni - Beef Dumplings

Filling Ingredients:

1 pound ground beef
1/2 tbsp. kosher salt
1/2 tbsp. ground black pepper
1/2 onion, grated

Dough Ingredients:

1 cup all-purpose flour
1 pinch kosher salt
1/2 cup hot water
1 tbsp. canola oil

Garnish Ingredients:

1 chopped green onion
1 stalk fresh dill, chopped
Kosher salt and ground black pepper
Sour cream, for serving

Directions:

1. For the filling: Combine the beef, salt, pepper and onion in a stand mixer fitted with the paddle attachment and slowly mix together.
2. For the dough: Line a baking sheet with parchment paper and set aside.
3. Add flour and salt to the cleaned bowl of a stand mixer and slowly mix.
4. Add water and oil.
5. Mix completely. Knead the dough into a ball, then roll into a log shape.
6. Slice a thin piece of dough and roll into a thin 4-inch round.
7. Place 1 tbsp. beef mixture in the center of the dough circle.
8. Fold circle into a half-moon and seal the edges. Bend the dumplings while pinching center and bringing the edges together. (Shape will be similar to a tortellini.) Place on the lined baking sheet.
9. Repeat with remaining dough and filling. Refrigerate for about 10 minutes to help them hold their shape.
10. Bring a large pot of salted water to a boil.
11. Add dumplings; they will rise to the top once they are finished cooking.
12. Plate and garnish with fresh green onion, dill, salt, pepper and sour cream.

Vareniki - Potato Dumplings

Filling Ingredients:

1/2 onion, chopped
Oil, for cooking
1 potato, boiled in its skin until tender, then peeled
1/2 tbsp. kosher salt
1/2 tbsp. ground black pepper

Dough Ingredients:

1 cup all-purpose flour
1 pinch kosher salt
1/2 cup hot water
1 tbsp. canola oil
Garnish:
1/2 chopped onion
Oil, for cooking
Kosher salt and ground black pepper
Sour cream, for serving

Directions:

1. For the filling: Sauté onions with oil in a pan until softened and brown.
2. Grate warm potato into a bowl and add the sautéed onion, salt and pepper.
3. Mix together to evenly distribute ingredients into a mash-like mixture.
4. For the dough: Line a baking sheet with parchment paper and set aside.
5. Add flour and salt to the cleaned bowl of a stand mixer and slowly mix.
6. Add water and oil.
7. Mix completely.
8. Remove dough and work into a roll, then a log shape.
9. Slice a thin piece of dough and roll into a thin 4-inch round.
10. Place 1 tbsp. potato mixture in the center of the dough circle, then fold circle into a half-moon and seal the edges.
11. Place on the lined baking sheet.
12. Fold over the edge of the dumpling, like a pot sticker.
13. Repeat with remaining dough and filling. Refrigerate for about 10 minutes to hold their shape.
14. Bring a large pot of salted water to a boil.
15. Add dumplings; they will rise to the top once they are finished cooking.

16. For the garnish: Caramelize onions in some oil in a frying pan until golden brown and crispy, 5 minutes. Plate dumplings and lay caramelized onions on top with salt, pepper and sour cream.

Ukrainian Hot Chocolate

Orange Creme Fraiche Ingredients:

1/2 cup creme fraiche
1 tsp. brown sugar
Finely grated orange rind, to taste

Pudding Ingredients:

1/3 cup sugar
2 tbsps. cornstarch
1 1/4 cups heavy cream
1 1/4 cups milk
1 vanilla bean, split
7 oz. bittersweet chocolate, chopped
3 tbsps. butter

Directions:

1. Make the Orange Creme Fraiche: Combine all the ingredients in a chilled bowl and whisk until soft peaks form.
2. Chill until ready to serve.
3. Make the Pudding: In a bowl whisk together the sugar and cornstarch to blend.
4. Whisk in the cream, milk, and vanilla bean.
5. Pour mixture into a stainless steel saucepan and bring it to a boil, whisking, until thickened, about 4 minutes.
6. Remove the pan from the heat and whisk in the chocolate and butter until melted. Fish out the vanilla bean and rinse it.
7. Wrap the vanilla bean in plastic wrap and refrigerate for another use.
8. Pour the hot chocolate into warmed demitasse cups and serve immediately with dollops of the orange creme fraiche served on the side on demitasse spoons.

Red Radish Salad

Ingredients:

2 tsps. sugar
1 lemon, juiced
1/2 cup sour cream
8 red radishes, thinly sliced
2 Delicious apples, quartered cored and thinly sliced
1/2 European seedless cucumber, thinly sliced
2 tbsps. chopped fresh dill
Salt and black pepper

Directions:

1. Combine sugar, lemon juice, and sour cream in a medium bowl with a fork.
2. Add radishes, apple, and cucumber.
3. Turn vegetables and fruit in dressing to coat.
4. Season with dill, salt, and pepper, toss again; serve.

Blinchiki

Ingredients:

3 eggs
1/2 tsp. salt
1 soup spoon sugar
1 cup milk
2 cups flour
1 splash of vegetable oil

Directions:

1. Mix the eggs, salt and sugar until thoroughly blended.
2. Stir in 1 cup of milk.
3. Add flour until a thick batter is formed.
4. Add a splash of vegetable oil to mixture.
5. Pour the batter into a hot, oiled skillet.
6. Fry until golden on 1 side, then flip over and brown the other side.

Chicken Kiev

Ingredients:

Vegetable oil, for frying
4 (6 to 8-oz.) pieces boneless, skinless chicken
2 tbsps. fresh chives, chopped
2 tbsps. fresh parsley, finely chopped
2 tbsps. fresh dill, finely chopped
1 clove garlic, finely chopped
6 tbsps. chilled butter
1 cup flour
2 eggs
1 cup plain bread crumbs
1 wedge lemon
Salt and pepper
Plain, round toothpicks

Directions:

1. In a large, deep skillet, heat 1 1/2 inches vegetable oil over medium high heat.
2. The oil needs to be 360 degrees F for frying.
3. If you do not have a frying thermometer, add a cube of white bread to hot oil.
4. If the bread browns in a 40 count, the oil is ready.
5. Cover work surface with waxed paper.
6. Arrange breasts on paper.
7. Butterfly small chicken breasts, cut into flesh and across, but not through the breast, and open them up.
8. The 6-oz. thin cut breasts may just be removed from package and arranged on waxed paper.
9. Cover breast meat with a second sheet of waxed paper.
10. Pound out cutlets to 1/4-inch thick with a small heavy skillet or a rubber mallet. Be careful not to tear meat.
11. Roll up waxed paper and breasts and set aside.
12. Combine chopped herbs on cutting board with chopped garlic.
13. Cut 4 (1 1/2 tbsps.) pieces of cold butter and coat each piece liberally with the herb garlic mixture.
14. In 3 disposable pie tins, set out flour, eggs beaten with a splash of cold water and bread crumbs.
15. Uncover chicken and squeeze a wedge of lemon over breasts.
16. Season chicken with salt and pepper.
17. Place an herb-covered piece of butter on each piece of chicken.
18. Wrap and roll cutlets tightly up and over the butter cubes. Discard pie tins used for breading.
19. Secure stuffed chicken with toothpicks.

20. Roll stuffed breasts in flour, then egg, then bread crumbs.
21. Fry the Kiev bundles 7 to 8 minutes on each side until deep golden brown all over.

Ukrainian Cherry Teacakes

Ingredients:

1 cup unsalted butter
1/2 cup confectioners' sugar, plus more for rolling
1 tsp. vanilla extract
2 1/4 cups all-purpose flour
1/4 tsp. salt
3/4 cup finely chopped pecans
1/2 cup candied glace cherries, chopped

Directions:

1. Cream the butter, sugar, and vanilla thoroughly. Sift together the flour and salt, add to the butter, and mix.
2. Fold in the nuts and cherries and chill the dough for 1 hour.
3. Preheat the oven to 400 degrees F.
4. Roll the dough into 1-inch balls and place on an ungreased cookie sheet (they do not spread as they bake).
5. Bake until set but do not brown, about 10 minutes.
6. While still warm but set, roll the cookies in confectioners' sugar and cool.
7. Roll in confectioners' sugar again and bake again for 10 to 12 minutes.

Halushki

Ingredients:

1 recipe dumpling dough, recipe follows
4 tbsps. butter
2 cups julienne onions
Salt
Freshly ground white pepper
1 pound cottage cheese
1 tbsp. finely chopped parsley leaves
Dumpling Dough:
2 cups water
2 tsps. vegetable oil
1 egg
1 tsp. salt
3 to 4 cups all-purpose flour

Directions:

1. Bring a pot of salted water to a boil. Turn the dough out unto a floured surface.
2. Roll the dough out to about 14-inch rectangle and 1/4-inch thick.
3. Cut the dough into 1-inch squares.
4. Add the dough to the boiling water and cook for about 4 to 5 minutes, or until the dough floats for 1 minute in the water and is fully cooked.
5. Remove and drain on paper towels.
6. Season with salt.
7. Meanwhile, melt the butter in a large sauté pan.
8. Add the onions.
9. Season with salt and pepper. Sauté until tender, about 3 to 4 minutes.
10. In a large mixing bowl, toss the dumplings with the onions and cheese.
11. Toss well.
12. Season with salt and pepper. Spoon into a serving bowl and garnish with parsley.
13. Serve warm.
14. Dumpling Dough:
15. In a mixing bowl, combine the water, oil and egg.
16. Mix well.
17. Add the salt and 3 cups of the flour.
18. Mix until the dough comes together and form a smooth ball. **If the dough is too sticky-add a little more flour, about 1/4 cup at a time.
19. Cover with plastic wrap and allow to rest for 30 minutes.

Ukrainian Mushroom Soup

Ingredients:

2 cups dried mushrooms
8 cups cold water
1 clove garlic
1 tsp. salt
2 tbsps. chopped onion
1 tbsp. margarine or oil

Directions:

1. Break dried mushrooms into small pieces and rinse thoroughly with cold water to remove dirt granules.
2. Cover mushrooms with 8 cups cold water and add salt and garlic.
3. Cover and simmer for 2 hours or more until mushrooms are tender.
4. Add more salt to taste. When soup is done, sauté onion in oil and add to soup. Simmer for just a few minutes. Traditionally served Christmas Eve at Holy Supper.

Herb Buttered Noodles

Ingredients:

12 oz. egg noodles
2 tbsps. chopped flat-leaf parsley
1 tsp. chopped thyme leaves
2 tbsps. unsalted butter, room temperature
Kosher salt and freshly cracked black pepper

Directions:

1. Cook the noodles according to package directions in a large pot of salted boiling water.
2. Meanwhile, blend the herbs with the butter and salt and pepper, to taste in a large bowl.
3. Drain the cooked noodles and immediately add them to the bowl with the herbs and butter.
4. Toss and serve.

Potatoes and Onions

Ingredients:

1 1/2 pounds (about 3 potatoes) round, white thin skinned potatoes
1 large sweet onion
Coarse salt
1 tbsp. vegetable oil, 1 turn of the pan
2 tbsps. butter

Directions:

1. Heat a 10-inch heavy skillet over medium high heat.
2. Slice potatoes and onions very thin. Salt potatoes and onions.
3. Add oil and butter to the pan. When the butter foams, add potatoes and onions to the skillet.
4. Place a dinner plate on top of potatoes and weight it with any heavy object: a sack of flour, heavy canned goods, etc. Let the potatoes and onions crust, 2 to 3 minutes, then turn, replace weights, and let them crust again. Keep turning the potatoes and onions over for about 20 minutes, until they are evenly golden and crusted.

Ukrainian Honey Cake

Ingredients:

For the Burnt Honey:
3/4 cup wildflower honey
3 tbsps. cold water
For the Cake Layers:
14 tbsps. unsalted butter, cut into slices
1 cup white sugar
3/4 cup wildflower honey
6 large cold eggs
2 1/2 tsps. baking soda
3/4 tsp. fine salt
1 tsp. ground cinnamon
3 3/4 cups all-purpose flour
For the Frosting:
4 cups cold heavy whipping cream
3/4 cup sour cream

Directions:

1. Pour honey into a deep saucepan over medium heat. Boil until a shade darker and caramel-like in aroma, about 10 minutes. Turn off heat and whisk in cold water.
2. Preheat the oven to 375 degrees F (190 degrees C). Line a baking sheet with a silicone mat (such as Silpat®).
3. Place a mixing bowl and a whisk in the refrigerator.
4. Place a large metal bowl over the lowest heat setting on the stovetop.
5. Add butter, sugar, 1/4 cup of the burnt honey, and regular wildflower honey. Let sit until butter melts, 5 to 7 minutes.
6. Meanwhile, combine baking soda, salt, and cinnamon in a small bowl.
7. Whisk butter mixture and let sit until very warm to the touch.
8. Whisk in eggs. Keep mixture over low heat until it gets very warm again; whisk in baking soda mixture.
9. Remove from heat. Sift in flour in 2 or 3 additions, stirring well after each, until batter is easily spreadable.
10. Transfer about 1/2 cup batter onto the prepared baking sheet.
11. Spread into an 8- or 9-inch circle using an offset spatula. Shake and tap the pan to knock out any air bubbles.
12. Bake in the preheated oven until lightly browned, 6 to 7 minutes.
13. Remove liner from the pan and let cake layer continue cooling until firm enough to remove, 6 to 7 minutes. Invert cake onto a round of parchment paper.

14. Repeat until you have a total of 8 cake layers, letting each cool on an individual parchment round. Trim edges using a pizza wheel to ensure they are the same size; save scraps for crumb mixture.
15. Spread remaining batter onto the lined baking sheet.
16. Bake in the preheated oven until edges are dry, about 10 minutes.
17. Remove from the oven and cut into small pieces; toss with reserved cake scraps.
18. Return to the oven and continue to bake until browned, 7 to 10 minutes more. Let cool completely, 15 to 20 minutes. Transfer to a resealable bag and beat into fairly fine crumbs using a rolling pin.
19. Set aside.
20. Remove the bowl and whisk from the refrigerator.
21. Pour in heavy cream.
22. Whisk until soft peaks form.
23. Add remaining burnt honey and sour cream; continue whisking until stiff peaks form.
24. Place a cake layer on a parchment paper round on top of a pizza pan or serving plate.
25. Spread a cup of frosting evenly on top, almost to the edge.
26. Repeat with cake layers and frosting, pressing the layers in smooth-side down.
27. Place last cake layer smooth-side up. Frost the top and sides of the cake.
28. Cover with crumbs; clean any excess crumbs around base.
29. Cover with plastic wrap and refrigerate at least 8 hours, to overnight. Transfer to a cake stand using 2 spatulas.
30. Cut and serve.

Green Borscht - Spinach Soup

Ingredients:

64 oz chicken or vegetable broth
3 tbsp olive oil
1 medium onion minced
1 medium carrot grated on a large grater
3 large potatoes cubed
4 cups spinach chopped
1 zucchini cubed
3 tbsp lemon juice
4 egg hard-boiled and cubed (See the notes)
1/2 c parsley or dill chopped
Salt, pepper to taste
Sour cream for serving

Directions:

1. In a large pot or Dutch oven bring chicken broth to a boil and add potatoes.
2. Reduce the heat to medium low and cook for 15 minutes.
3. Meanwhile, heat olive oil in a medium non-stick skillet and on a medium heat.
4. Add onion and carrot and cook stirring occasionally for 10 minutes.
5. In a pot with potatoes, add sautéed onion, carrot, zucchini and spinach and continue cooking for 5-7 minutes.
6. Add salt and pepper to a taste.
7. Add lemon juice, cubed eggs and parsley.
8. Remove from the heat and serve immediately with a dollop of sour cream.

Buckwheat Kasha

Ingredients:

2 cups dried buckwheat groats
4 cups water (or broth)
1 tsp + 1 Tbsp butter
1 onion, diced
16 oz. cremini mushrooms, diced
3 cloves minced garlic
1/3 cup fresh dill, minced
1/4 cup fresh parsley, minced
Salt and freshly ground black pepper, to taste

Directions:

1. Rinse buckwheat groats 2 or 3 times in water; drain well.
2. In a large pot, melt 1 tsp of butter and a drizzle of olive oil.
3. Add groats and toast until fragrant.
4. Meanwhile, bring 4 cups of water to boil in an electric kettle. Alternatively, bring 4 cups of broth to a boil in a pot.
5. Add boiling water/broth to the toasted buckwheat groats. Careful, as the hot water hitting the hot groats will cause it to sputter wildly. It's important to add boiling water. If started in cold water, the buckwheat will be mushy.
6. Add a generous pinch of salt. Turn the heat to low, place a lid on the pot, and cook for 15 minutes.
7. After 15 minutes, remove from heat. Fluff buckwheat.
8. Cover with lid and allow to steam for an additional 5 minutes off the heat.
9. Heat 3 tbsp extra virgin olive oil. Add onions and mushrooms. Cook on medium-high heat, stirring constantly, until fragrant and mushrooms are browned and caramelized. Take the time to well caramelize the onions and mushrooms.
10. Add the garlic and continue cooking until the garlic is fragrant. Be careful not to burn it.
11. Add buckwheat. Heat through. Finish with 1 Tbsp of butter.
12. Season with salt, to taste. Add fresh dill and parsley and toss. Serve hot with sour cream or yogurt. Great as a side or main dish. Leftovers freeze well.

Pozharsky Cutlets

Ingredients:

1 1/2 lb. ground chicken
1/2 cup heavy cream
4 slices of white bread plus 5 more slices for breadcrumbs
1 big yellow onion
2 eggs
1 tsp dried parsley
salt and freshly ground pepper
4 tbsp. olive oil
5 tbsp. butter

Directions:

1. In a medium bowl, place the slices of white bread and pour the heavy cream over them. Let it soak for 10 minutes until they become soggy.
2. Set aside.
3. In a large bowl mix together ground chicken, dried parsley, salt, and pepper.
4. Add the onion to the food processor. Chop well.
5. Mix the chopped onion, soggy bread with the ground chicken.
6. Add the eggs to the chicken mixture and mix very well.
7. To make homemade breadcrumbs: Pre-heat your oven to 300F. Trim crusts from the rest of the white bread.
8. Cut bread into small cubes and spread them on a rimmed baking sheet; bake until crumbs are a little dry, 15 minutes.
9. Take them out and turn the oven to 350F, you will need to use the oven later.
10. Take a handful of chicken mix, make an oval-shaped cutlet with wet hands, put a small piece of butter (about 1/2 tbsp.) in the middle of the cutlet, and close the cutlet using your hands.
11. Adding the butter is necessary to get a juicy cutlet.
12. Roll the cutlet in breadcrumbs, and fry with olive oil in a preheated skillet for about 2-3 minutes per side.
13. When all the cutlets start to turn a golden brown color, place them in a preheated to 350F oven for about 10-15 minutes.
14. Serve one cutlet per serving, with roasted potatoes, pickled beans or other vegetables of your choice.

About the Author

Laura Sommers is **The Recipe Lady!**

She lives on a small farm in Baltimore County, Maryland and has a passion for all things domestic especially when it comes to saving money. She has a profitable eBay business and is a couponing addict. Follow her tips and tricks to learn how to make delicious meals on a budget, save money or to learn the latest life hack!

Visit my Amazon Author Page to see my latest books:

amazon.com/author/laurasommers

Visit my blog for even more great recipes:

http://the-recipe-lady.blogspot.com/

Follow me on Pinterest:

http://pinterest.com/therecipelady1

Follow me on Facebook:

https://www.facebook.com/therecipegirl/

Follow me on Twitter:

https://twitter.com/TheRecipeLady1

Other Books by Laura Sommers

Microwave Mug Meals

Easter Cookie Recipe

St. Patrick's Day Cookie Recipes

Christmas Cookie Recipes

German Christmas Cookbook

Recipe Hacks for Sriracha Hot Chili Sauce

Flavored Compound Butter Recipes

Recipes Using Turmeric Spice

Homemade Salad Dressing Recipes

Copycat Restaurant Sauces and Spices Cookbook

Printed in Great Britain
by Amazon